BIG RIGS

BIG RIGS

ON THE ROAD WITH THE WORLD'S BEST SEMI TRUCKS

BETTE GARBER

This edition published in 2004 by Crestline,an imprint of
MBI Publishing Company, Galtier Plaza, Suite 200,
380 Jackson Street, St. Paul, MN 55101-3885 USA

The information in this book is true and complete to the best
of our knowledge. All recommendations are made without
any guarantee on the part of the author or Publisher, who
also disclaim any liability incurred in connection with the use
of this data or specific details.

We recognize that some words, model names and
designations, for example, mentioned herein are the
property of the trademark holder. We use them for
identification purposes only. This is not an official
publication.

Crestline titles are also available at discounts in bulk quantity
for industrial or sales-promotional use.
For details please contact Special Sales Manager
at MBI Publishing Company, Galtier Plaza, Suite 200,
380 Jackson Street, St. Paul, MN 55101-3885 USA.

ISBN 0-7603-1996-0

CREDITS
Photography © Bette Garber

Editor: Lesley Wilson
Designer: Cara Hamilton
Production: Don Campaniello
Reproduction: Anorax Imaging Ltd

Printed and bound in Malaysia

*My heartfelt thanks to the owner
of the splendid International 9300 on
the cover. You make the trucking
industry look good.*

Contents

INTRODUCTION *page 6*

FREIGHTLINER *page 42*
VOLVO *page 90*
INTERNATIONAL *page 104*
KENWORTH *page 132*
MARMON, STERLING & AUTOCAR *page 222*
PETERBILT *page 240*
MACK *page 348*
WESTERN STAR *page 382*

INDEX *page 398*
ACKNOWLEDGMENTS *page 400*

Introduction

What are rigs? They are trucks that transport goods throughout America, working the road 24/7. They are restored classics and showpieces. They are rolling canvases of personal expression upon which owners create works of art through paintwork, metal shine, and lighting. Rigs are a range of mighty machines, each with individual specifications and features to fit the job at hand. Working the rigs is a lifestyle choice for the owners and drivers. This book is all about diesel-powered haulers, the transport wagons of the 21st Century. Slide into the culture of Big Rigs, and take the ride of your life.

Left: This 1998 Century Class Freightliner rides on a 24in wheelbase. Over 100 lights run around the fenders and fairings a glitzy accompaniment to the rippling vinyl graphics.

Left: A smaller size integral sleeper Volvo 420. This versatile Volvo is well-suited for regional bulk haul applications. Its sloped hood and large, one-piece windshield give it panoramic visibility for safer driving. ABS brakes are a standard safety feature.

Opposite: Typical assignment for the Western Star 4964 model is pulling a drop deck trailer loaded with large, heavy equipment.

Everyone notices when a big truck goes by, whether you're a truck enthusiast, a seasoned expert, a trucker yourself, or the person standing on the side of the road or watching from a window. Except for trucks being very large vehicles (that are hard to miss!), what is it about big rigs that captures our imagination and fuels diesel dreams? Perhaps it's the bright colors of customized vehicles or the squeaky clean tractor that seems to defy its purpose. It might be the draw of shiny tankers that reflect the surrounding desert or waterside, or chromed and lit-up tractors and trailers. The combinations and varieties are amazing—a special, beautiful, productive creation resulting from the meeting between man (and woman!) and machine. Whatever it is, I love it. I have been photographing trucks for more than twenty-five years and not tired of them yet.

This book is a celebration of trucks. The text and pictures are divided into chapters that attempt to cover the great and the good of transport tractors: Freightliner, Volvo, International, Kenworth, Marmon, Autocar,

Above: An International 9300 tractor, pulling a refrigerator trailer. This shot offers a nice view of the side of this model, speced with the 72in Hi-Rise sleeper.

Opposite: A Peterbilt 359. Look on the chip guards under the headlights to see the Peterbilt logos that the owner has placed there. There is also a light bar mounted under the bumper.

Sterling, Peterbilt, Mack, and Western Star. It encompasses the old and new, fleet trucks and owner–operator land cruisers, the plain as well as the customized. These fascinating vehicles have been captured on American highways, at truck shows, in quarries, by the dockside, and in the snow, the rain, and the sun. They tend to be awash with color and some are decorated in strikingly individual ways with personally commissioned murals and graphics of great power and beauty. There are those that enjoy shiny accessories and dazzling light displays. Many trucks are literally rolling works of art, so beautiful that people often find it hard to believe that they actually pull loads from coast to coast.

Each truck has individual specifications that are put together to allow the vehicle to do what it's supposed to

do—whether that be hauling timber on a flatbed, lettuce in a reefer, or chicken feed components in a hopper. There is no way to know the details of every truck on the road, but wherever possible, basic specifications for the pictured bobtails (tractor only) and combinations (tractor–trailers) have been provided: model, engine, horsepower, transmission, and rear end ratio, and sometimes with a description of location, interstate, or the stories of their owners.

The Heart of Transport

Trade routes have existed since civilization began and with them have been the means by which goods and people have been transported. It could be said that the people who drove wagons and carts were early truckers, and that the twenty-first century has replaced the oat-fed horses with fuel-fed steeds. Today's horsepower is computerized and environmentally friendly.

Left: In northern California the sight of giant logs cradled in spiked log trailers is a familiar one. Many of the trucks hauling logs are privately owned and operated Peterbilts like this one, an obviously well-maintained Model 379 with a sharply chromed bumper.

Transmissions vary, as likely to be a 6-speed Allison Automatic as a Fuller 18-speed manual. Technology has advanced, allowing instant communication between truck and home base and increasing the ability to find a truck on the highway. Sensors tell a trucker how close to the dock he is and on-board systems can weigh the load. There are night-vision cameras that transmit to an inside screen, cameras to tell a driver when a car is alongside, ergonomically designed dashes and steering wheels, and seats that vibrate, massage, and adjust infinitely to support the driver's spine. The trailers that these steel steeds pull are certainly bigger and more specialized but in concept they are still wagons and modern truckers continue to use the word "wagon" as an affectionate reference to their trailers.

Opposite: A spectacularly painted Mack, a cut down recreation of a B model built by reknowned custom builder George Sprowl.

Below: Just as nature abhors a vacuum, a Mack trucker fills an R model Mack's empty fender with custom lights.

The main purpose of trucking remains the transportation of goods. Truckers go where the freight is, pick it up, and take it to where it needs to go, which means trucks often look anything but pristine: in the summer, bugs make a mess of paint and windshields, they get into grilles and plug up the radiators; in winter, highway "slop" deposits a chalky residue that combines with salt, dirt, and chemicals to cause havoc on electric wiring and the trucks' appearance. Truckers pray for rain and a free rinse. In contrast are the immaculate rigs at truck shows, so clean and polished you could eat a meal off their fenders.

The most popular owner–operator models in my files are the "Hoods," the Kenworth W900B and W900L models, along with Peterbilt 379s and 359s, and Freightliner Classic XLs. The sight of a big hood thrusting out ahead of the windshield seems irresistible to truckers. Of all the hoods, the leanest and meanest are the out-to-there restored "needle-nose" models from the '50s, '60s, and early '70s. This doesn't, however, discount others that, in this book, include a Mardi-Gras-themed Western Star and Volvo 770s.

21st Century Trucking

From equipment to communications, trucking has stepped firmly into the future, putting to use all that technology offers in response to rising fuel prices, pollution concerns, business competition, government regulations, and manufacturer incentives to provide the

Opposite: Dawn on a lonely interstate with big rigs silhouetted against the lightening sky. Truck in front is a Peterbilt 379 extended hood and behind it, a Kenworth W900L.

Right: A cheerful cab interior and sleeper. The truck is a 1997 W900L Kenworth called *Sadie*.

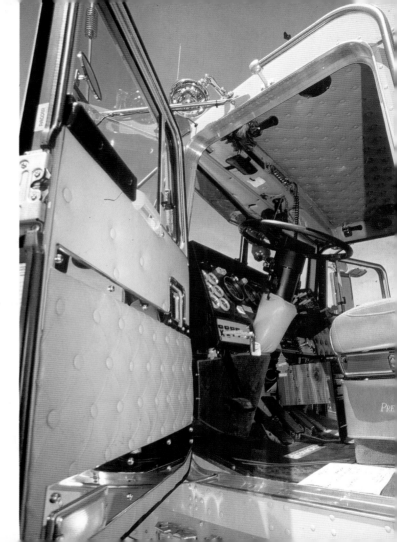

best ride for the buck... and the job.

Back in the 80s, Kenworth introduced what could be called the first aerodynamic tractor, the T600. Truckers scoffed, calling it an "anteater" or "aardvark" because its hood curved towards the highway instead of jutting firmly into the wind. Its cab was aluminum, lightening the rig's overall weight. And it didn't take long before savvy truckers were embracing this new breed of tractor for its increased fuel efficiency. Today, every truck manufacturer offers heavy duty power-units (tractors) designed to minimize air resistance—the Kenworth T2000, Peterbilt 387, Mack Vision, International's 9000*i* Series, Volvo's VN 610, 660, and 770, Freightliner's 3 C's (Columbia, Century, and Coronado), and Western Star's Low-Max and Constellation.

With fuel prices steadily rising, truckers want any edge available. These days that edge is sculpted and curved on hoods, mirrors, fenders, and fairings. The less a truck has to fight the wind, the better mileage it will

Right: A 42-wheeled Michigan giant, a Freightliner FLD 120 teamed with a double set of dump trailers. Gross weight on these "Michigan trains" can climb beyond 150,000 lbs.

Above: Clearly a lot of thought went into setting up this tri-axle dump truck photographed at the Mid-America Trucking Show. Note the air wings on hood and fenders, custom bumper and visor, and stainless inserts and abundance of red lights.

Opposite: Just because a truck hauls cement doesn't mean it can't look good, like this Peterbilt at a concrete batching plant.

get. While Big Hood models continue to attract "old-school" buyers, the death knell for the Big Hoods might be ringing on the fuel pumps. The lighter-weight, aerodynamically-enhanced tractors may finally convince even "Billy Big Rigger" to abandon the hefty "Hood" for a more fuel-efficient mode of highway transport.

In response to pollution concerns, plumes of black smoke no longer waft from shiny stacks; today's exhaust gas recirculation (EGR) engines burn fuel cleanly, with barely a trace of particulates to be found in their emissions. Emissions guidelines that became effective on 1st October 2002 required all new heavy-duty, on-highway engines to meet strict standards which will become even more restrictive in 2007. The promise for this technology is cleaner air, cleaner engines, and, hopefully, better fuel

Above: Twice the beauty, *Streaker* is reflected in a pond on Dick Johns' farm. The powerful image of stampeding horses grabs the eye and makes it impossible to look away.

economy down the road.

Computer technology under the hood means that it is increasingly difficult, if not impossible, to "tinker" when things go wrong, but it does mean that today's diesel truck engines have efficient operation and ease of maintenance. To diagnose an engine problem, today's diesel "doctor" (technician) simply wheels a computer up to the truck, plugs it in, and downloads the stats.

Industry-wide communications have undergone a similar change. Trucks can be tracked by satellite and a customer can access instant GPS positioning on the internet to follow the progress of their load. Truckers stay in touch using long distance two-way radios and camera-phones, through satellite-linked computers, even computer hookups with camera attachments. To find loads to haul in the past, truckers would

Below: Strong graphics combine unfurled racing flags with images of snarling big cats. This is a 2001 Kenworth W900L Studio sleeper.

Above: Neon lights in green and gold glimmer from every corner at night.on this 1996 W900L

Below: The restored beauty of this vintage B 61 model Mack. The nose and fenders all demonstrate the distinctive rounded look of the B model.

line up at truckstop telephones to contact freight brokers or carrier dispatchers. Now, company drivers and lease operators can access their carrier's website to find backhaul loads and independent brokers can also make loads available using the internet.

Visibility and, in direct relation, safety, has increased with the emergence of LED (light emitting diode) lighting into trucking in 1989. Truck lights are brighter, sharper, and their extraordinary brilliance is a big safety factor. LEDs outlast incandescent lamps by a factor of ten and current draw is low, using five percent of the energy of a regular incandescent bulb. The bulbs last up to ten years. Unlike incandescent light, which takes two-tenths of a second to reach 95 percent of full brightness, LED light produces 100 percent output in ten nanoseconds, that is, instantly.

Inside the cab and bunk, manufacturers have ratcheted up the comfort level to keep drivers happy both on and off-duty. The "coffin" sleepers of yesterday are no more. Walk-in, stand-up sleepers in a variety of heights and lengths come loaded with amenities that provide home-style comfort. All in all, the trucker is receiving a safer, more comfortable, ride.

With such a promising start to the new century, the future of highway transport can only get better.

Restoring

Restoring a truck is a popular pursuit—and you can see why. To many older truckers and fans of seasoned equipment, restoration is a way to keep these venerable rides out on the highway where they belong—at the head of a trailer, chewing up the blacktop, and delivering freight. "You can buy a good lookin' new ride, but you have to make a good-lookin' old ride" says one owner–operator who goes on to praise the all-metal rides of yesteryear over the increasing use of plastic and

Right: A Volvo VN 610 integral sleeper just sings with style as it comes across Wyoming pulling a fan trailer.

Above: This is a Peterbilt 379 pulling a 48ft van trailer through the snow with consummate skill and patience.

composite materials. When a trucker rejects a newer model in favor of restoring and working an older model, he honors his roots in the business and is understandably proud of the accomplishment. A working restoration is the mark of a long-time long-hauler, often someone who actually drove the equipment years ago, when it was new. Sometimes, the restorer is simply knocked-out by the designs of yesteryear and the only way to get one is... to find an old one and make it yourself! Some of the older models in this book are on the road but many have been retired and only venture out for compliments and trucking event trophies.

On the road

As racking up the miles is the most common way to make money in this profession, drivers usually choose to stay on the road for weeks, even months... a long time to be away from home. This is why a significant number of owner–operator tractors in this book have stretched-out wheelbases, which accommodate oversize custom sleepers that are equipped with all the comforts of home (the big bunks, as long as 12ft and up to 102in wide).

Right: A truck travels the great in-between: between coasts, between borders, and often the only vehicle seen for miles.

Now even the biggest fleets are commissioning new tractors with the latest comforts for their drivers— pullout work stations, power inverters and electric outlets, generators, extra storage, and dedicated space for televisions, microwaves, and coffeepots. This move to comfort is, in part, a response to the newly revised and federally mandated US Hours of Service requirements. Increasing the comfort factor also helping to attract and keep drivers.

Combos

A wide range of working trailers and truck bodies can be teamed with the tractors to make the "combination" or full "rig." Reefers (refrigerated trailers) primarily carry fresh and frozen foods, pharmaceuticals, computer hardware, or any commodity requiring exact temperature controls. Flatbeds (open and side-kit styles plus drop decks) transport lumber, steel bars and coils, pipes, and all manner of machinery and equipment,

containers, vehicles, hay, and even fresh produce. Tankers (baffled and unbaffled, bottles and pneumatic) haul liquid and dry commodities including plastic pellets, fruit juice, flour, chemicals, and gases. Livestock wagons tow cattle, sheep, and pigs. Dump trailers and bodies unload from the back or from the belly ("belly dumps" or "hoppers"); they haul grain, rocks, and produce. Specialty vans come equipped with custom interior and exterior storage for transporting household goods, entertainer tours, and even luxury autos and racecars. Finally, the most familiar is the dry van, which is used to carry all sorts of dry freight including artwork, furniture, and clothing.

Trucking and truckers

Long haul trucking, the central focus of this book, is very much a way of life and a state of mind. For a trucker, every day offers a new destination, new people to meet, sights to see, and new challenges to conquer with no storefront or office to report to. It is said that people pay to go to all the places that truckers are paid to go to. The world of the trucker is seen by its citizens

Opposite: A Peterbilt 357 cement truck. This model has been highly popular with construction trucks because of the many ways that the truck can be set up for specific types of hauling.

Below: This owner-operator rig pulls a chemical tanker through a rain storm in Ohio with a nicely striped and lighted Peterbilt 379 long hood model.

as an extended community—the neighborhood is 3000 miles long. Often long-haulers will see people they know on the Pennsylvania highways, catching up with them again several days later in California. Friends pass along the major routes, but not so fast that they can't pass a greeting on the CB (citizens band) radio before

Above: You don't want to be standing next to this outfit when all the noisemakers go off. A shiny cluster of air horns crowns the cab on *King of the Road*, a 1980 Kenworth W900A. Behind the bunk an array of (very loud) train horns is mounted on the deck as well.

they run out of range.

Many drivers, these days, are women. According to the US Bureau of Labor Statistics in 2000 4.7 percent of truck drivers were female. In 2001, the number grew to 5.3 percent, and their numbers are continuing to increase. A number of trucks in this book are owned and operated by women, some as singles, others as part of a married team.

Truckers have a tremendous amount of responsibility. Big rigs normally weigh 80,000lbs and heavy haulers can obtain permits to carry more than twice that, and it takes a skilled a professional to control this weight in heavy traffic (in or out of town), coming down mountains, or maneuvering around dangerous bends. In the US, the professional driver brings to the job a hard-earned Commercial Driver's License (CDL) and road-honed skills for keeping the truck upright and between the ditches. With this responsibility comes the understanding that truckers will drive through all weather, over weekends and holidays, and even forego their own family to get the job done. There is a popular saying among truckers: Without trucks, America stops.

This is a truism—trucks are the arteries through which American commerce flows.

Operating a trucking company, however large or small, is an expensive operation and exacts a heavy price with rising road taxes, fuel prices, insurance, and highway tolls. Truckers employ many tactics to save money, often taking on just enough fuel until they can drive to where the fuel prices are lower and they can fill up the tank completely.

It's not all open-road glamour of course. Fermenting fish meal in a Georgia feed mill in August and the loading and unloading of animals, specifically in stockyards, feed lots, and meat packing plants with biting flies, can have smells that make you gag . Whether the load is sheep, "short legs" (market size pigs), or "long legs" (cattle), the miseries concerned are a reluctantly accepted part of the trucking

environment.

This book shows trucks in an enormous array of locations, from stockyards and construction sites to

Below: A 9300 Eagle truck is broken down anywhere near Bloomington, Ill., count on this fiery red specialized International recovery truck owned by Southtown Wrecker Service, Inc. to come to the rescue.

Left: A hunk of chrome underlined with a stainless light bar dresses up a CL600 long nose conventional Mack. The bumper is a highly unusual find on a tri-axle dump truck.

Opposite: Both blue-ribbon winners, these two Kenworth W900L bobtails are dressed to impress with custom paint, lots of lights plus custom stainless and chrome accessories.

quarries, farms, warehouses, docks, and forests; in other words, everywhere and anywhere trucks pick up and deliver the goods that drive the nation's economy.

Stylin' and Profilin'

A truck's appearance is a source of pride for its owner. Truckers call it stylin' and profilin' and it is a significant measure of one's mark within the industry. Customization sets trucks apart from their diesel brethren and customized trucks present a clean, colorful, distinctive (easily recognized), and professionally maintained face to their clients. For fleets and owner–operators, a customized truck makes a good impression on their clients. Furthermore, once a client has the rig stuck in their mind it is more likely that they'll request the same truck for repeat pickups because they can remember that it was the one with "Gone With the Wind" painted on the side. Every owner–operator rig is a work in progress. As the owner refines the ideas that make the truck unique, so the truck changes and they just keep getting better with age.

Fleet show trucks take stylin' and profilin' to new heights. These rigs are pet projects of trucking company owners, and their employees, and few limits are placed on customization when building them. At night the

Below: Classic Peterbilt 379 owner-operator rig is dressed up with lights and chrome bumper to give these autos a good-looking ride.

sizzling display of lights and customization are guaranteed to make awestruck onlookers stare. Although most of the lovingly painted and illuminated fleet show trucks are only for exhibition, a few do actually carry freight.

Truck stories

People of all ages, from all walks of life, are drawn to the mystique of the big rigs. These giant gypsies of the highway appear larger than life as they pound the pavement between two coasts. The events that occur on these journeys and the people that are involved are fascinating. Truckers stories could go on for hours. Here are a few.

Whereas many people lack the opportunity to experience big rigs up close, others find ways to get a closer look. A Pennsylvania trucker

Above: Abundance of louvers adds visual interest to the hood, giving it that sought-after "different" twist that truckers favor.

was driving a gasoline tanker, delivering fuel to service stations. While unloading, a hefty grandmotherly woman, waiting for her husband to gas up, left her car and approached the trucker with a request—could she look inside the truck cab? This was no ordinary truck, but a sky-high Ford CL9000 cabover. Entry was achieved via a steep ladder up the side of the tractor. And so it came to pass that a woman in a voluminous flowered dress, hauled herself up the ladder, assisted by a push from the rear by the driver (and this author). "This looks like an airplane cockpit", she wheezed cheerily, out of breath from the climb, "I always wanted to know what it looked like inside!"

Truckers whose rigs are heavily customized are frequently photographed by "civilians" as they roll down the highway. One owner–operator couple whose truck feature artwork honoring the victims of the events of 9/11 is accustomed to people coming up to them in rest areas and even on the streets for a closer look. Some on-lookers are overcome with emotion and walk away with tear-streaked faces.

One doctor left her practice to become a truck driver. It was while watching rolling rigs on a nearby highway, clearly visible from her office window, that she caught the legendary "white line feever," closed up shop, and went to truck driving school. She couldn't wait to trade in her white lab coat for jeans, boots, and a cowboy hat. When her employer learned she was an MD, he convinced her to come off the road for a few days each month to do drivers' physicals in the company clinic, but for the rest of the month she is a long-haul truck driver.

Left: On a bitter cold January day this Western Star's grille is warmly winterized with a cozy quilted winter front.

Truck World and the photographer

The trips I have taken have been long and strange, often taking me to some unusual places to pick up goods. One such stop was a chicken processing plant in Natchitoches, Louisiana where chickens were killed processed, packaged, and frozen. The truck I was accompanying pulled into the facility well after midnight and backed up to a loading dock, in preparation for picking up a trailer-load of frozen poultry parts. From the "shotgun seat" and under a huge yellow moon I watched a line of open carts filled with live chickens being wheeled into the plant; one lone, white bird tried, and failed, to escape. They disappeared into the building to be transformed into headless, naked carcasses, spinning about on metal wheels in a cavernous room as white and bright as a hospital operating theatre. The chicken parts we picked up went west to become part of the menu in a well-known chicken specialty restaurant in Los Angeles.

On another trip, in the rugged hills that mark out the Russian River Valley of California, I accompanied truckers who were picking up cases of wine from a vineyard that was so remote it could only be accessed by doing three takes on a double blind S-curve. It was October and clusters of beautiful purple grapes hung heavy on the vines while I photographed a magnificent Kenworth combination, silhouetted against rustic vineyard buildings.

Freedom

This diesel-driven world has been my creative focus for more than a quarter of a century and continues today. To acquire photographs I put myself into the truckers' world, traveling throughout the US on their rigs, always with proper authorization, and photographing the equipment and drivers in their working environment. I share their lifestyle: dining on fast food, taking a number to wait for a shower, and even finding medical services. I have also driven the highways coast to coast on my

Right: The owner of this Peterbilt dresses up the front of his long nose Peterbilt with lots of custom metal accents.

own with just two dogs for company. There is no denying the outsiders' attraction to the trucker mystique, who would not want to be free to drive anywhere, at anytime, with no one looking over their shoulder? The desire to be similarly unencumbered, if only in one's own mind, is hypnotic but, in reality, is no longer true for today's truckers.

Before the advent of satellite and cellular tracking, long haul truckers boasted about their freedom to do a job without anyone telling them how to do it. As long as the load got delivered on time, little attention was paid to how the driver got it there but this is no longer the case. Today, the eye in the sky can tell exactly where most trucks are and record how long they stop for. The new working rules further cut into the drivers' sense of freedom but, as long as truckers can learn to adapt their

Left: The look of the aerodynamically designed Peterbilt Model 387 is all high style, from its stylish curves to dramatically sculpted grille and headlights. It definitely adds class to the dry box it's pulling.

Opposite: A beautiful Peterbilt 379 extended hood with a double stack of lights under the front slab of chrome, a lineup of lights on the chip guards, and low-key graphics.

operations within the confines of the new laws, the job should continue to offer unlimited new horizons, new challenges, and daily self-determination unparalleled in most other occupations.

These newly imposed controls on trucking, however, will never stop legions of armchair trucking devotees and impressionable youths from dreaming of "Rubber Duck's" call to run off with a convoy. The mind's eye will continue to call forth images of dawn-kissed horizons, the exquisite ballet of reverse blind side parallel parking, and the passage of thousands of big rigs in the night, marked only by a ribbon of golden marker lights. Now, step into *Rigs*. It's time to go truckin'!

This book is dedicated to my beloved bearded collie, Boo, a dog-pound mutt that grew up to travel America and joyfully water some of this country's finest truckstops and rest areas. He was by my side when many of these photos were taken. Boo died on April 23,

Above: A red 1990 Peterbilt Model 379 short hood, teamed here with a 1990 Cobra 30ft box (31ft frame) tri-axle dump trailer.

Left: Whistle-worthy two-tone Peterbilt 379 and polished out aluminum tanker, part of Texas-based Steere Tank Lines, is looking its best having just taken part in the Truckers Jamboree in Walcott, Iowa. This shiny rig transports flammable products.

2004 and is deeply missed. I wish to express my gratitude to the truckers who contributed to this project and in particular to George Steigerwalt, Freightliner of Philadelphia, Roger Gerhart and John Hoppes, Gerhart Equipment Co., Inc., and John Walsh, Mack Trucks.

1 Freightliner

There is something about a Freightliner: at once solid, attractive, declaring its reliability and purpose. Every Freightliner is custom built. Buyers choose from seven different sleeper cabs, three engines, and a dizzying array of comfort and luxury options. It is one of only a few manufacturers still building a cabover.

Left: A 2001 Freightliner Classic XL 132 is a rolling light show with a chromed and stainless pieces, and added lights.

Below: A Freightliner Classic XL with 70in raised roof, set up with accent lights and an air wing on its hood, churns the rain beneath its wheels. The truck's title comes from its impressive 132in BBC (bumper to back of cab).

Opposite: Heavy equipment is just one of the many types of freight transported on a flatbed, in this case pulled by a powerful extended-hood Freightliner Classic XL with 70in raised roof.

Below: A Freightliner Classic XL with a 70in raised roof sleeper cab pulls a "No Zone" trailer. Inside, with a wraparound dash and full set of standard and optional gauges, command of the incredible power of the Classic XL is at the driver's fingertips.

Above: A Freightliner FLD 120 combo. The Pennsylvania owner–operator did all the lighting himself. It starts with Freightliner's 120in BBC (bumper to back of cab) conventional with a set-forward front axle. The truck can be speced with a variety of sleeper options including 40in and 60in sleeper boxes, 48in and 70in sleeper cabs, and fixed or fold down bunks.

Left: A Freightliner FLD 120 with set-forward axle and flatbed trailer. Its popularity is based on its appearance, performance and comfort, high-horsepower capacity, and technologically advanced components.

Below: The Freightliner FLD 120 tractor, teamed with a van trailer, is a fleet favorite because of the many variations available to customize the model. For example, it is available as either a single or dual drive truck, with set-forward or set-back front axle, two sizes of sleeper box, three sleeper heights, and two integral sleeper cabs. The sloped hood, side fairings, and rolled under bumper help to heighten fuel efficiency.

Opposite: A custom chrome bumper enhanced with lights on a Freightliner Classic XL autohauler. The model has been Freightliner's top owner–operator truck.

Below: A Freightliner FLD 120 custom built with a big aftermarket sleeper added onto the 276in wheelbase. This truck even has heated fuel tanks and heated fuel lines. The bunk is loaded with homestyle amenities, including microwave, refrigerator, and TV.

Opposite: Freightliner Columbia mid-roof models seem to be everywhere. Particularly popular with flatbed and tanker carriers, this Columbia is pulling a step deck trailer. When setting up the truck, the buyer can spec diesel engines from 280-525hp. Engine manufacturers include Mercedes Benz, Detroit Diesel, and Caterpillar.

Right: Another Freightliner Columbia mid-roof fleet truck and van trailer. The standard leaf and a half front leaf spring suspension reduces weight by 20lbs over the two leaf design and improves ride quality. Weight savings are even better with the optional AirLiner front suspension which reduces weight by 96lbs over the 1.5 leaf suspension, and by 117lbs with standard taper leaf suspension.

Freightliner 2001 Classic XL 132

his 2001 Freightliner Classic XL132, an 18-wheeler customized ride from Trev Timblin in Wisconsin, should be slowly savored. This extraordinary Freightliner and 84in condo sleeper rides on a 300in wheelbase. The flooring inside the bunk is parqueted wood. Power comes from a 500hp Cummins working through an 18-speed transmission and 3.42 rear ends.

Below and right: Extraordinary colors with parquet wood inserts, chromed and stainless pieces, and added lights.

Opposite: The color-enhanced trailer is a 2001 Great Dane stainless van. The Michelin tyres are hand painted. See page 42 for a view of the truck with all lights blazing.

Left: A single axle Freightliner FLD 120. The set-back axle configuration on the tractor helps improve the driver's ability to maneuver in tight turns. The back axle is a single drive because what he hauls is not overly heavy. Also, the side mirrors are automated, sliding out to give a view alongside the wide load.

Opposite: A restored 1969 White Freightliner COE (cab over engine). Under the hood is a 250hp Cummins with Fuller 13-speed transmission and Eaton 4.31 rear ends.

Left: Wind rushes past this Columbia model Freightliner with less resistance and air drag thanks to the rounded curves on everything from mirrors to fenders to windshield which is sloped at an optimum angle of 24 degrees. A partial fender encloses the space above the front tire, again helping to improve aerodynamics, in addition to reducing road splash and contaminants reaching the engine.

Opposite: Freightliner's Columbia mid-roof model's design has attracted a loyal following as a result of the truck's responsive handling and aerodynamic styling which increases fuel economy. Add to that a comfortable interior and ergonomically designed dash for driver comfort. Maybe that's why the Freightliner reports the Columbia model has sold more than any other Class 8 truck in the industry in 2003.

Right: A Freightliner Columbia 70in raised roof tractor. This truck model offers all the strength and durability that Freightliner has built its reputation on along with many customizing options including 7 sleeper cab configurations, and the new 112in BBC configuration.

Opposite: This rig started as an off-the-lot tractor but owner-operator Bob Delaney transformed it into a freight hauler that stands out. The 1998 Century CS/T Freightliner with 70in raised roof rides on a 240in wheelbase. Over 100 lights run around the fenders and fairings, a glitzy accompaniment to the rippling vinyl graphics.

Right: This fleet hauler, a Freightliner Century CS/T with a 70in raised roof sleeper cab, pulls a 53ft van trailer through heavy traffic. Freightliner's most technologically advanced truck to date, the Century CS/T was engineered to improve fuel economy, provide ease of maintenance, and prolong the truck's life expectancy.

Above: This 1986 Freightliner Classic XL 132 is painted with patriotic murals. The 338in wheelbase truck tips the scales at 24,500 pounds. Engine is a 3406B air-to-air 425hp Caterpillar. The 6 x 4 Spicer (1241D and 1263A auxiliary) tranny paired with 3.90 Eaton rear ends.

Right: A detailed view of the 132 (above), The long hood plus the 144in custom sleeper provides a broad canvas filled with images of fighter jets, tanks, ships, and flags. More than 100 marker lights accent the murals and give the bobtail a spectacular illumination at night.

Classic XL Limited Edition

Powerful graphics and a brilliant display of lights give Jim Thomas' Classic XL Freightliner a fierce presence. This 2001 Classic XL Limited Edition Freightliner is powered with a 500hp Detroit, 13-speed Eaton transmission, and 3.70 rears. The wheelbase is 275in. Inside the 84in raised roof sleeper cab the Native American-inspired decor is accented with rosewood and native art pieces. *Sacred Fire* sets the night ablaze with 94 lights, including 6-light rock guards, 22-light chrome bumper with the truck's name laser-cut and back lit, and 3-light air cleaners.

Below: The flame and phoenix motifs dominate outside.

Above: Ruby Red Pearl Metallic blazes on white, accented with yellow and red vinyl flames and gold leaf lettering.

Below: This combo, a Freightliner Columbia tractor, features the 70in raised roof sleeper with side and top windows. For driver comfort there are EzyRider® seats designed to Freightliner's specs that adjust front to back, up and down, with air lumbar support.

Above: This combo is a Freightliner Century CS/T with 70in raised roof sleeper cab pulling a refrigerated trailer. Driver amenities include a lowered wrap-around dash design, backlit LED gauges, individually lighted flipper and rocker switches, and switchable indicator lights. Foot-activated steering column adjustment is optional.

Opposite: A patient Freightliner Century CS/T and intermodal container. The Century here is speced with a 70in raised roof sleeper cab. A driver can feel confident that the aerodynamic design, coupled with innovations like a patented under-the-hood air management system and SmartShift, will provide exceptional handling and fuel efficiency.

Left: A Freightliner Century CS/T tractor pulling a "dry box." Strong, lightweight components in the hood and fenders reduce overall weight of the cab, allowing for increased payload capacity. Sleeper is a 70in raised roof, but the truck is available in six other sleeper types as well as day cab.

Opposite: The Freightliner Century CS/T 70in raised roof, here pulling a pair of van trailers, is popular with drivers and fleet managers for its aerodynamic design and other design innovations that contribute to driver comfort and fuel efficiency.

Below: A customized Freightliner Century CS/T 70in raised roof pulling a moving van. The truck comes standard with anti-lock brakes, driver-side airbag, a first aid kit, and fire extinguisher.

Above: A two-tone look is pulled off with panache on this Freightliner Century CS/T with 70in raised roof sleeper cab, pulling a van trailer. Enhancements to this popular Freightliner include the two-piece curved windshield, large convex mirrors, and a choice of painted or chrome grille designed to increase airflow and optimize cooling efficiency. Composite headlights provide widespread light distribution over the road surface.

Opposite: A load of pipe piled on a flat top Freightliner 120 flatbed combo makes its way through a crowded truckstop at dusk.

Below: A Freightliner Century CS/T flat top pulling its load into the night. Advanced noise reduction technology throughout the cab creates a quieter interior. Cab suspension front and back is specifically set up to reduce road vibration and improve the ride.

Right: A Freightliner Century CS/T 70in mid-roof sleeper is arguably one of the most popular seen on US highways. The sleepers allow even tall drivers to fully stand up, come with two bunks, and an assortment of options to customize the truck.

Classic XL 132

This 1995 Freightliner Classic XL 132 has been transformed over every inch of body and frame. Note the custom headlight bar, shaved fenders, and the old-style headlights. Riding a 290in wheelbase, the long nose conventional boasts a custom bunk, wood floors, custom billet aluminum accessories, and rosewood paneling. Engine is a 500hp Detroit Series 60 with an Eaton Fuller 15-speed overdrive tranny, and 3.58 Rockwell rears.

Right: This rig pulls a reefer trailer transporting meat throughout the country.

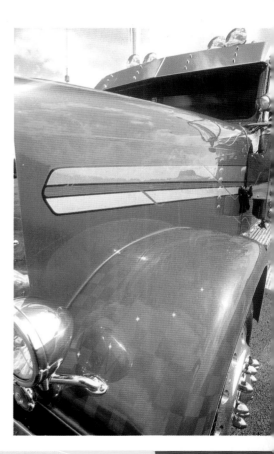

Above and Right: Subtle but stunning checkered fenders match similarly painted brake drums. The motor and suspension are chromed. Over $250,000 worth of customization makes this ride unique.

Left: Enormously popular fleet workhorse, the Freightliner Century CS/T with 70in mid-roof sleeper, here takes a curve with a shiny white dry van in tow. A 50 degree wheel cut on this model allows for tight maneuvering and backing. The new Detroit Diesel Series 60 EGR (Exhaust Gas Recirculation) Engine is rated up to 500hp and is standard on the newest Century Class S/Ts. Powerplant options from 280 to 500 horsepower include diesel engines from Mercedes-Benz, Detroit Diesel, and Caterpillar.

Opposite: The Century CS/T is easy to maintain, thanks to starship-level technological enhancements. The truck is equipped with a Data Logging Unit that records important information—such as road speed, engine parameters, throttle position, and clutch and brake status — before and after a problem or accident, for future diagnosis. Freightliner's ServicePro® software helps technicians diagnose problems quickly and accurately, so the vehicle spends more time on the road and less time in the shop.

Below: A 2000 Freightliner Classic XL and 53ft Manac 2000. Over 500 Truck-Lite LEDs light this beautiful combination.

Opposite: A 2000 Freightliner Classic tri-axle dump truck. Ther e is interesting studding on the front of the fenders, lights on the bumper, and flourishes of contrast color striping. This heavy-duty hauler shoulders loads of sand, gravel, and earth products

Right: An long haul Freightliner FLD from the Eighties with a side-kit flatbed filled with onions makes a stop on its way east. This tractor wears the embellishments of an owner–operator, from the shiny visor to the chrome bumper.

Below: A long hood Freightliner FLD 120 truck pulls a field box plus extra pup trailer hauling tomatoes to a processing plant in California. The sloped hood angle, rounded roof and fairings, sculpted fenders and rolled-under bumpers, even the exterior visor improve the truck's aerodynamics and increase its fuel efficiency. Interesting fact: to remove the tomatoes, the boxes are filled with water and the tomatoes floated out onto conveyor belts.

Opposite: In the summertime, trucks like this Freightliner FLD 120 flat top slams on double field trailers and loads up to race fresh-picked ripe tomatoes to canneries for processing.

Opposite: *Plum Crazy*, an FLD 120 fronting a triaxle dump, hauling five or six loads of stone daily, putting on 80,000 to 100,000 miles a year within one state. Under the hood, a 400hp Big Cam IV Cummins backed by a 13-speed Fuller RTO-14613 transmission carried this Freightliner dump truck up and down Maryland's mountains and quarries.

Left: Embellishments to this tri-axle dump include chrome bumper, grille, and dual straight pipes. Pinstripes and additional lights gave it even more style.

Opposite: Freightliner Classic and bulk trailer are at one with the highway, the tandem drive tires clearly rolling this combination towards its destination.

Right: Stanley and Irene Strang and their sons specialize in transporting liquid soap in squeaky-clean stainless steel tankers pulled by beautifully appointed blue tractors like this 1984 Freightliner on a 300in wheel base. Their typical haul is 5,000 gallons in a one-compartment (unbaffled) tanker. Their son Dave drove this set up with a then-experimental electronic DDEC-1 8V92 Detroit (475hp) with the electronic Allison.

Freightliner Fleet

John Bunning Transfer Co., Inc. was founded in Rock Springs, Wyoming in 1895 by Peter Christian Bunning and his son John. The Bunning fleet evolved to a stable of silver gray Freightliners, FLD 120 conventionals, cabovers, and day cabs. Engines in the fleet are (at time of photograph) 400hp Detroit Series 60 and Cummins engines, driving through 13- and 15-speed transmissions. Trailers are a mix of flatbeds, pneumatic dry bulk trailers, and insulated tankers.

Opposite: A load of molten sulfur is on its way to the fertilizer plant, south of Rock Springs pulled by a daycab Freightliner. A derivative of natural gas separated out during processing, molten sulfur is transported in insulated tankers at 300F. To prevent burns from splashed sulfur, drivers wear gloves, goggles, hard hats, long-sleeved shirts, and air-breathing apparatus while loading and unloading as a precaution against hydrogen sulfide gas which occurs naturally in sulfur production.

Left: Long and short haul operations are built on regional natural resources: petroleum (servicing oil-field rigs), mining (hauling various forms of soda ash) and power generation (transporting molten sulphur, a natural gas by-product). At the time of this photograph in the mid-Nineties the fleet was solidly Freightliner, conventionals and day cabs.

Above: A bright green 1990 Freightliner FLD 120 with hot pink striping and a "K" of lights (owner's name Ken Zwald) on the grille. Milk rides in a pair of stainless steel Brenner tankers.

Opposite: A 1995 Freightliner Classic XL 132. The sleeper is a 70in flat roof on a 265in wheelbase. Base color is Champagne Pearl Metallic. The frame is Bright Violet Pearl Metallic. A 455hp Caterpillar 3406E provides the power. Transmission is a 10-speed overdrive with 3.73 rear ratio. Over 100 LEDS add sparkle. Stainless steel bumper is a 20in Texas square. It pulls a 1969 liquid tanker hauling ammonium chloride.

Left: A 1991 dark blue FLD 120 model on a 240in wheelbase. Under the hood is a 430hp Detroit Diesel engine with 13-speed double overdrive transmission. Stylish touches include the stainless bumper and 110 lights. Foodliner trailer is a 42ft Heil pneumatic tanker for hauling food-grade products, in this case, flour.

Below: A bulk tanker teamed with a sharply painted and lighted Freightliner Classic XL132. The heavy duty Classic XL houses the capacity for the biggest engines on the road and flaunts the biggest hood on the highway: an imposing 132in BBC.

Opposite: A classic Freightliner cab-over-engine (COE). (Freightliner are one of the few truck makers who still offer a COE model). This is the non-sleeper model, custom built to the customer's specifications and featuring rigid frame design, front springs, an aerodynamic design, and a large flat windshield for excellent visibility.

2 Volvo

Originating from Sweden, Volvo trucks have been around since 1927. The company's first diesel powered vehicle was introduced in the late Forties and in the following decade this manufacturer was dominating fifty percent of national truck sales. Today Volvo is the third largest producer of trucks world-wide. Volvo's VN series of working trucks, and the VHD (Volvo heavy duty) series are highly visible on US highways, city streets, construction sites, and off-road locations. The Volvo is most popular with fleets but offers amazing power combined with luxury for owner–operators.

Left: A fleet Volvo VN 610 takes a curve pulling a 48ft standard dry van trailer. These are the trucks that make up a large part of truck transport across America: built for the long haul, with plenty of style, comfort, and fuel efficiency.

Opposite: Rolling through a truckstop at the day's close, this well-traveled Volvo flat top tractor shows its age with a split windshield and its headlight design.

Below: An intermodal container pulled by a diesel-powered tractor workhorse Volvo VN day cab. This model delivers fuel efficiency in both city and highway driving. With a 50 degree wheel cut and 23ft turn radius it makes maneuvering a breeze. The sloped hood offers an expanded view of the road.

Left: A Volvo VN 610 tractor and refrigerated trailer. Driving the VN 610 is an experience underscored by comfort, with air-ride suspension and a high-back seat that features horizontal, vertical, and lumbar adjustments. Engines can be selected from all popular makes; some dealers offer an off-the-lot model powered by Volvo VE 345hp engine.

Right: A 1999 Volvo VN 770, with fish, bubbles, and beaches. Under the hood of *Sea Dreams* is a Detroit Diesel Series 60 550hp engine with Eaton 18-speed Autoshift and 3.55 rears. Trailer is a Great Dane Thermacube 48ft van.

Below: Patriotically striped Volvo VN 610 medium roof tractor is a popular choice for fleets doing regional and drop and hook hauling as well as over the road transport because of its size, component choices, and accommodating interior. In this photo the VN 610 is teamed up with a flatbed. One sure way to spot this model is the lack of a side window behind the cab.

Above: Satellite antennas on a Volvo VN 610. No longer isolated from the world, truck drivers like those in this truckstop, can stay as entertained and informed in their trucks as well as they can in their own living rooms.

Opposite: This powerful Volvo VN 770 and matching van trailer is enhanced with a custom chrome bumper and stainless light bars down the side. The interior on this model Volvo is among the most luxurious, offering a choice of double bunks or a dinette that converts into a bunk, automatic climate controls, roomy storage compartments, and a wardrobe cabinet. In the cab is an ergonomically designed dash and steer column with controls (cruise, high beams, turn signals, windshield) located on the column.

Volvo VN 770

This truck is a 1999 Volvo VN 770 powered with a Cummins Signature 600 with an 18-speed double overdrive transmission and 3.55 ratio rears. The VN Series offers a variety of popular engine makes, including the Volvo VE D12 featuring a 5 year/500,000 mile warranty and 200-600lbs weight savings. The integrated cab and sleeper area provides more than 50 square ft of living area beneath an 8ft ceiling.

Right: This mural on *Miss Wendy II* (preceded by *Miss Wendy*), was hand painted.

Above: Microscopic prisms in the paint create a unique effect of changing colors as the viewer changes position and the light changes angles.

Opposite: Lightweight, but exceptionally rigid HSS (High Strength Steel) welded cab construction is standard on the latest models.

Left: The Volvo VN 420 integral sleeper here pulling a refrigerated trailer is a versatile vehicle: lightweight, hard working, and fuel efficient. The roomy interior stretches 74in from the windshield to the back of the cab. It also comes equipped with three overhead storage compartments, and convenient under-the-bunk storage.

Below: This Volvo VN 660 high roof has a comfortable integral sleeper which includes a pull-out work area. The fleet truck pulls a van trailer.

Opposite: A handsomely designed Volvo VN 660 integral sleeper, known for its aerodynamic styling, high safety standards, and state-of-the-art technology. Other features include the LED digital displays on the dash, a new electrical system, SRS air bag protection, and an Air Conditioning Protection and Diagnostics System that alerts the driver to AC system problems in advance of costly repairs.

Right: This Volvo VN 660 integral sleeper tractor, pulling a matching white trailer, features an aerodynamically styled roof fairing. The one-piece windshield and dramatic slope to the hood provide an enhanced view of the road.

3 International

International heavy trucks are synonymous with long hauling, style, and comfort. The International diesel engine is the heart of the company and their market includes both medium- and heavy-duty trucks. The good-looking, driver-pleasing models include a long nose 9900*ix*, aerodynamic 9200*i*, the popular 9300, and many others, all with enough spec. choices to make a potential owner confident of getting exactly the truck needed to get the job done.

Left: The stars and stripes fly over a proudly and independently owned and operated International 9300 Eagle with 72in. Hi-Rise sleeper. This Eagle pulls a moving trailer for National Van Lines.

Opposite: This is a 1998 International 9300 Eagle teamed with a 2002 EBY walking floor trailer, with an eagle on the hood and planes and flags on the trailer.

Right: This 1952 International Harvester cabover with gull wing hood was worked up until the 1980s and completely restored by the owner. Each side of the hood open independently of the other.

Opposite: This impressive 1999 Dark Red Metallic International Eagle 9300 on a 250in wheelbase is outfitted with a 20in Valley Chrome bumper, over 100 lights. Engine is a 450hp Caterpillar 3406E with 13-speed transmission and 3.55 rears. This beauty pulls a drop deck trailer, transporting John Deere tractors one way and steel coils or bricks on the back haul.

Below: This 1979 4070B Eagle Transtar II was rescued from a junkyard. The sunny air-ride cabover is powered by a 400hp Cummins, 13-speed transmission and 3.70 rears. It pulls a 1989 48ft x 96in Dorsey reefer and transports honey, flowers, and meat throughout the US.

Above and Left: A working antique, this 1965 Emoryville International A model named *Paradise* is owned and operated by Mike and Lisa Jones, the truck's third owner. The engine is a Caterpillar.

Opposite: Oversized construction equipment on a drop deck trailer is chauffeured by an International 9900*i* model tractor, a classic conventional with chromed front end and a comfortable 72in Hi-Rise sleeper with an aerodynamically shaped roof that directs air up and over the trailer and helps improve fuel economy.

Opposite: A 1999 International Eagle 9400 set up with a 500hp Caterpillar 3406E, 13-speed Fuller, and 3.44 rears. The 18in bumper is loaded with 76 bulbs.

Right: There are 600 lights on the tractor overall. The wolf theme honors a beloved Norwegian Elkhound named "Buck," now deceased.

Above: A tarped flatbed with side-kit teams up with this 9300 International with 72in Hi-Rise Pro Sleeper. A flatbed side-kit (stakes and panels) added to a flatbed offers versatility and the ability to haul a larger variety of loads. The kit can be put up or removed fairly quickly, providing the trucker the ability to haul bulk products as well as bars, pipes, machinery, just about anything amenable to a strapped down ride on a flat surface.

Right: A Great Dane trailer teamed with an International 9400 tractor. From this angle you can appreciate the slope to the sculpted hood, part of an overall aerodynamic design that contributes to better fuel economy.

Below: The driver of this International 9300 pulls his trailer through the colorful foliage of northwestern Pennsylvania.

Left: An International Eagle 9400 with Pro Sleeper Sky-Rise integrated sleeper cab pulls a flatbed through West Virginia. This model can be speced with a single or double bunk sleeper. In the cab is 69in of stand-up room, and 90in in the bunk area.

Opposite: The New Jersey truck picks up cocoa beans from cargo ships and transports them to a chocolate company for processing. This Forest Green Metallic 1998 International Eagle 9300 has an 70in sleeper pulling a 40ft Ravens end dump trailer with 9ft spread. Under the hood is a Cummins N14 252hp engine with Fuller 18-speed transmission and Meritor 3.9 ratio rear ends.

Left: An International Eagle 9300. Inside the 72in Pro Sleeper are wraparound shelves, a deep wardrobe, and ample storage under the bunk. The Owens Corning insulation package helps maintain the inside temperature while making the cab exceptionally quiet.

Below: One of a fleet of Internationals pulling refrigerated trailers. This truck model was a special edition and, as with other limited designs by International, this one features unique eagle-inspired graphics along the cab sides.

Opposite: An International 9300 Eagle with lights that run along the step as well as along the bunk, cab, and bumper.

International Eagle

Auto parts are transported in style in this 1982 International Eagle and 2002 53ft stainless Great Dane dry van. The tractor is powered by a 475hp Big Cam 3 Cummins twin turbo engine with 13-speed Eaton double overdrive and Rockwell 3.70 rears. Wheelbase is 297in.

Above: Flooring is ceramic tile for easy maintenance and it looks terrific. Custom stainless, including a stainless dash, and wood pieces add to the unique styling of this Eagle's interior.

Left and opposite: After dark this combo glitters with more than 350 Truck-Lite LEDs. Imagine the delight of late night viewers who see this comet blazing through the night on its dedicated run between Indianapolis, Iowa, and Erie, Pennsylvania. Purchased in 1994, this truck has hauled 1,800,000+ miles.

Left: A 1986 International Eagle 9300 day cab and refrigerated 48ft Great Dane stainless trailer. Power comes from a 400hp Cummins with 10-speed Fuller transmission. Owner Norman Mahoney painted a small leprechaun dancing a jig just below the refrigerator unit.

Opposite: An International 9400 Eagle with a 72in Hi-Rise sleeper, and set up with a flatbed. The stock bumper has been replaced with a custom chrome slab underlined in lights on a stainless bar. The chrome-bezeled headlight/turn signal assembly comes standard on this model.

Below: From this angle it is easy to see the generous sweep of the roof directing the air up and over the trailer. The truck is an International Eagle 9000 Series tractor pulling what appears to be a dry van.

Above: A 1996 International 9300 pulling a 1996 Utility Refrigerated van. Power comes from a 500hp Caterpillar 3406E, Fuller RTLO-18718B 18-speed double overdrive and a 3.58 rear ratio.

Opposite: This old International cabover truck works as a farm truck outside Bakersfield, its field trailer box transporting watermelons in from the field.

Right: A flatbed trailer on an International Eagle 9900*i* tractor. This model truck delivers a long hood design featuring a chrome grille, headlight bezels, and full-width bumper, all with the requisite shine. Horsepower on this model can go up to 600.

Left: This 1989 International 9300 cab is the handiwork of Mike Duffy, from the flames on the outside to the flames on the plexiglas cab floor that lets through neon light, purple of course, from under the truck at night. This truck doesn't haul loads. It just looks good. And that makes its owner very happy.

Right: If you think Mike Duffy's 1989 International 9300 looks good during the day, imagine how it looks at night with all these lights on—a fiery jewel that rivals the heavens for star power.

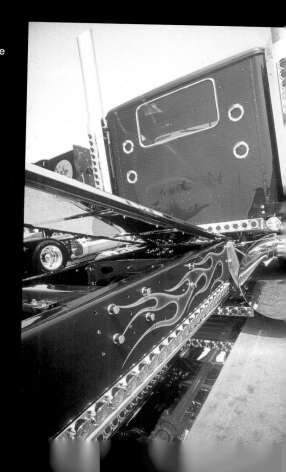

Below: International 9100 day cab and wagon train is loaded with tomatoes photographed during the late summer "crush," the race to get the tomatoes to the canneries.

Opposite: Dump Deluxe, a tri-axle 1997 International 9400 Eagle, with lights along the dump body and bumper, hauls stone, sand, and salt in eastern Pennsylvania.

Above: An International 9000 series day cab pulling a flammable placarded load. Internationals are popular for hauling dry bulk, liquid, or compressed gas products.

Left: A red International 9900 tractor pulling its trailer load of milk. The distinctive headlight bezel is chrome-plated with built-in turn lights, a definite signature characteristic of this model.

Opposite: Liquid tanker gets a smart ride from this two-toned International 9400 with a 51in sleeper. This model can be speced with dual 80- or 100-gallon fuel tanks.

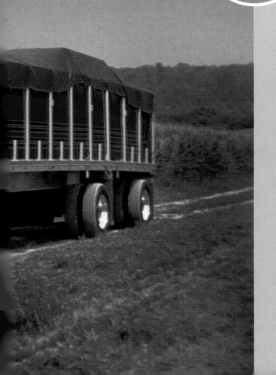

4 **Kenworth**

Founded in 1923, Kenworth tractors are among the most popular makes riding America's highways. Drivers and owner–operators enjoy the truck's handsome looks, such as the long hood of the W900 models or the sloped hoods of the T600 and T2000, the quality construction, ergonomic dash configurations, cab layouts, and dependability. Kenworth's cowl-mounted mirrors and sunroof cabs are also popular.

Left: A Kenworth W900 and side-kit flatbed. The sides can be removed and the trailer used for loads that do not require containment.

Opposite: The longest stripe in the world, or so it seems (4 blues and a burgundy), on a 1994 W900B Kenworth with big custom bunk sitting on a 300in wheelbase. Matching trailer is a 2001 Kentucky moving van.

Below: A pennant of racing flags adds extra flair to an already magnificently appointed Kenworth W900B pulling a Reliable Moving & Storage trailer.

Opposite: A Kenworth model 800 preparing to take on a load of cattle ("long legs"), a heavy and unstable load that need the hefty shoulders of this set-back axle conventional.

Below: 2000 Kenworth W900L Aerocab "Thunder Struck." The 285in wheel base tractor wears over 100 Millennium lights by Panelite and pulls a 2002 53ft Kentucky "Mover Plus" trailer with three axles. Power comes from a 600hp Cummins engine with 18-speed transmission and 3.55 rear ends.

Below: A red metallic 1998 T2000, with artwork of an American Eagle flying across the stars and stripes.

Above: A 998 T2000 Kenworth, a magnificent shackeled eagle artwork on the side. This model is the next step up from the T600 model (see below).

Opposite: Set in the grandeur of New Mexico's rugged mountains, this bright red Kenworth T600 and whistle-clean trailer heads west on Interstate 40. The model is extremely durable and gets excellent fuel mileage—all attractive features for large fleets.

Opposite: This W900L Kenworth was designed by owner–operator Bob Sunderland. Forward trends include the duotone with darker color on fenders and tanks, and gold leaf trim. For this trucker the Kenworth was the only make to consider for coast-to-coast hauling.

Right: Everything about this Kenworth looks good—from the hot rod lights and early Turbo Wing to the back wall mural.

American Pride

This 1998 W900L Kenworth. The TV satellite dish is chromed. Custom neon light boxes on trailer end light up with "WHOA" or "THANK YOU."

The trailer is a 1996 stainless steel Dorsey dry van. Custom chrome and stainless steel accessories and numerous lights elevate this showpiece into a class all its own.

Right: *American Pride* has murals with a distinctly American theme, this one featuring the Statue of Liberty.

Opposite: A mural entitled, "These Colors Never Run," a dramatic American eagle soaring across a starred and striped field.

Below: Neon lights glimmer on the W900L from every corner at night.

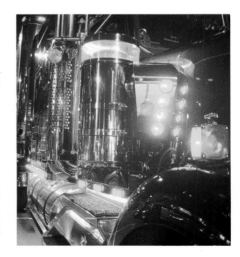

Opposite: This smartly pin-striped owner–operator outfit is a Kenworth W900 with classic sleeper box and flatbed. Note the polished chrome rims.

Below: A Kenworth T600. The logo for Amazon Transport is a fearless female warrior holding a leash with four trucks on broken chains. It says that owner-operators prefer to operate independently.

Left: *Simple Pleasures* is anything but a simple truck. The simple specs: 2001 Kenworth W900L on a 292in wheelbase. Diesel horses are 500 strong in an ISX Cummins with 13-speed transmission and 3.36 rears. This beauty pulls bulk pneumatic and liquid tankers. Illinois trucker Buzz Sweeden has given it style, dazzled it with light and shine, and dressed it with custom pieces, like the unique laser-cut grille and air cleaner inserts.

Opposite: A nicely dressed Kenworth T600 pulls a load of cars across Wyoming. The tractor was the first in Kenworth's line with aerodynamic styling that resulted in demonstrable operating economy by delivering exceptional fuel mileage.

Opposite: This 2001 Kenworth T2000 is awash with intense coloration on the nose and murals inspired by the famous movie, "Gone With The Wind." The Utility van is covered in murals depicting scenes from the film. Neon light bars down the side and under the trailer are spectacular to see at night. When this truck is at a show, the entire Butler clan and crew parade about in Civil War-era dress, from top hats and cutaway tails for the men to voluminous gowns and parasols for the women.

Right: This 1999 Kenworth W900L is a rolling advertisement for Kelvin and April Locklear's K&L Chrome Shop. Special features include suicide doors with embossed flamed upholstery, wood floors, racing seats, stretched stainless deck, and lights everywhere. The couple take this showpiece on the road pulling a lighted-up trailer that opens on one side into a walk-up store offering all manner of dazzling automotive and truck accessories and lights.

Left: A colorful Kenworth T800. The heavy-duty T800 is a rugged, set-back axle conventional as popular in its time for off-road hauling as running freight.

Below: A working truck, this W900B Kenworth Aerodyne and refrigerated trailer look immaculate in a white and red palette. The accent color is carried through on the reefer, tank covers, and trims. The Aerodyne sleeper has been popular since its introduction, offering double bunks, and room for teams and couples to co-exist comfortably and to stand up and stretch. Extra light comes in through the topside roof windows.

Opposite: Medium Jade Green from bumper to bumper, this classic owner-operator combination 1984 W900B Kenworth and 1983 Utility reefer awaits a load of bananas on a Wilmington, Delaware dock.

Red Hot 'n' Rollin'

It's hard to beat this Viper Red 1989 Kenworth W900L and 1998 Trailmobile stainless trailer. The look of this classic long-nose truck and trailer is hot, the color even hotter. The truck was one of two specifically built to promote a "James Bond 007" movie. Wheelbase is a whopping 330in, the sleeper built and stretched by Kenworth, and is not aftermarket.

Above: The truck has special red and gold neon bars, all by Spectralite. The tractor weighs 29,000lbs the weight of some tractor-trailer combinations. Because of its weight, this truck rarely pulls loads. It just stands there and looks good.

Above: The stainless steel trailer adds shine to this good-looking rig which wears 11R22.5 Bridgestones all around that were recently replaced with Michelin X Super Singles.

Right: Red Hot 'n Rollin's power is an unheard-of 1600hp which comes from a Cummins KTTA bulldozer motor. Transmission is an 18-speed main and 4-speed auxiliary with 2-speed rear ends (highand low range).

Opposite: A Kenworth K100 Aerodyne VIT carries a specially built "drom" box behind the sleeper for stashing extra cargo. The paint scheme is extended all the way back to the box.

Above: A T800 model fronting a lumber-laden flatbed.

Left: This 1999 Kenworth W900L on a 270in wheelbase. They have combined the tractor with a 48ft 2001 Utility spread axle reefer.

Left: A Kenworth V100E VIT cabover. This model rides on a 180in wheelbase and is teamed with a 53ft Fruehauf trailer.

Below: Owner Keith Harring has acquired many of the Kenworth Limited Editions, like this one, the 1990 "James Bond 007" extended hood, a real beauty in white striped with black, trimmed with 18ft gold Kenworth medallions and outfitted with a $6000 sound system.

Opposite: The 1982 Kenworth W900A extended hood stands tall with 7in chrome straight pipes, lowered 6in overall. Wheelbase is 275in and engine is a 400hp Caterpillar 3406A with 15-speed transmission. It pulls a 48ft by 102in Great Dane reefer transporting fresh produce between the east and west coasts.

Big Engined W900Ls

Two trucking bluebloods, Deep Regatta Blue to be exact, are owned and operated by Connecticut trucker Chris Fischer. Both trucks are Kenworth W900L models with the Studio Sleeper, speced with big 600hp Caterpillar engines. They earn their living pulling flatbeds loaded with machinery and heavy equipment.

Opposite: The Kenworth W900L is a standout, from the array of 88 lights to the long pennant of racing flags flying from front to back. The extended hood is 10in longer than the W900B.

Left: Wild flames reminiscent of curved knives lend an element of danger to Chris Fischer's 2003 W900L Kenworth. The sleeper on the truck features Aerodyne styling with windows on the side but a stainless panel instead windows on the roof.

Right: A 2003 Kenworth W900L Studio sleeper model. There are 136 lights overall on the bobtail. On this model Kenworth emblems are located right behind the fender, not seen on the W900B. Headlights blend smoothly into the fender and into a chrome-plated steel bumper.

Opposite: On this Amazon Transport trailer, the long-tressed warrior rides the winds on the back of a giant pterodactyl. The tractor is a W900B Kenworth embellished with some pinstriping and extra lights.

Above: A matching Kenworth W900 tractor and refrigerated trailer. Tire of preference on this rig is Bridgestone which the owners have hand painted.

Left and below: Asbury Trucking, Dayton, Ohio, has a winner in this 1999 Kenworth W900L on a 290in wheel base, hosting an 86in studio sleeper. The muscle to move this beauty is a 550hp Caterpillar with 18-speed transmission and 3.55 Eaton rear ends.The custom LED lights on this Kenworth W900L were installed by owners Jerry and Allan Asbury to highlight the distinctive lines of this popular Kenworth model. Additional neon lighting by Spectralite gives this truck an edge at night. Inside is a 1000 watt Alpine stereo.

Opposite: The 1997 W900L Kenworth powers up with a 500hp Detroit Diesel backed with a 13-speed Eaton transmission. It pulls a 53ft refrigerated trailer hauling temperature-controlled and dry freight throughout the US.

Below: A hard-working 1999 Kenworth W900L out of Minnesota, this diesel hauler charges across 48 states and Canada with a 565hp Cummins under its hood. It transports flour, sugar, and dry food products in a pneumatic trailer.

Above: Details on this W900L (left) include 110 lights and flame motif on the fuel tanks.

Opposite: A magnificence T600 Kenworth with a stretched out wheelbase, an immense custom bunk, and lavish light display. This model was known as the Anteater when it first debuted in the late '80s because of the sloped nose.

Above: The T2000's distinctive grille, and its aerodynamic package makes the Kenworth T2000 not only easy to identify. The sleek good looks, spacious interior, and tight handling are all popular with drivers as is fuel mileage, crucial to a fleet's bottom line.

Opposite: A Kenworth T2000 and van trailer. This tractor model is popular with fleets for its weight savings and fuel efficiency. Better visibility through the large windshield, and the shorter hood, improves driving, and a tight turning radius makes it easy to handle.

Above and Right: Montana livestock hauler Rob Gilbert transports hogs, cattle, and sheep with this 1991 W900B Kenworth painted high-voltage red, glittered with gold accents, with lots of chrome accessories and added lights. Gilbert's trailer is a 1986 Wilson drop center livestock transporter with three decks that accommodate over 200 market hogs.

Opposite: This majestic, beautifully lighted combination fronted by a 1983 Kenworth W900B is the fleet flagship of Pride Transport, Salt Lake City, Utah.

1997 Custom W900L

This 1997 W900L Kenworth sits on a 310in wheelbase which holds the oversize sleeper. A powerhouse 550hp 3406 Caterpillar hosts an 18-speed double overdrive Fuller transmission with a 3.70 rear ratio. The 22in chrome Texas square bumper is underlined with a chrome rail from a pickup truck. At night green neon tubes glow inside the air cleaners and 109 lights lend requisite razzle-dazzle. The tractor weighes 21,340lbs with half tanks of fuel, water, and possessions, and 41,000 pounds of cargo could go in the trailer.

Left: A spectacular full length stripe patterned after the chrome line of a '57 tail-finned Chevy extends front to back. Predominant color is Dupont Imron Salmon with Lime Green and Boysenberry accents.

Opposite: This truck hauls office furniture west and fresh produce east in a 53ft reefer.

Below: Night lights rule on a classic, illuminated W900 (left) standing fender-to-fender with a Peterbilt 359 (right). Both trucks are long-haulers pulling refrigerated trailers.

Opposite: A Kenworth W900B and refrigerated trailer stands out with lots of neat custom touches, like Kenworth medallions on the air cleaners, quilted tank covers, and extra lights on the bumper.

Left: Parading down Virginia Street in Reno under the famous arch, this wildly flamed Kenworth is a working truck, running between California and New York state every week. This special transporter is drenched in cartoon colors inside and out, with purple leather seats, and hot pink and chrome yellow accessories. Shown here as a bobtail, this 1999 Kenworth W900L Studio sits on a 270in wheelbase. Under the flamed hood, the engine is a 600hp 3406E Caterpillar. Transmission is an 18-speed Fuller with 3.55 rear ratio. Their 2000 Dorsey 48ft, 102in spread axle reefer trailer is painted to match with an 8ft orange flame down each side.

Opposite: On the same Kenworth W900L, Dark Violet Metallic teams with white, plus Hot Pink Pearl on the frame. Distinctive air-brushed teardrop flames in Pearl Orange, Yellow, White, Dark Purple, and Hot Pink are accented with Lime Green and Bright Blue.

Right: Chromed rooster on the hood is a nod to the truck's status as a "chicken hauler," that is, a fancy, typically independent, owner–operator's ride.

Left: A 2000 Kenworth W900L standing on a 300in wheelbase and pulling a 48ft Utility spread axle refrigerated trailer. Engine is a 550hp Caterpillar C-15 with 13-speed transmission and 3.42 Rockwell rear ends. Bumper is a hefty 22in Texas square.

Below: The combo lights up the night with a total of 249 Truck-Lite LEDs. The W900L hauls frozen food and produce south to Florida and brings fresh seafood back to Wisconsin.

Below: This 1992 W900L Kenworth is a standout in shades of rose and wine with gold accents. With a wheelbase of 265in, this heavy hauler boasts a 425hp Caterpillar with 15-speed transmission and 3.70 rears. Trailer is a 48ft by 102in Great Dane spread axle reefer. The truck hauled produce between Florida and the northeastern markets.

Opposite: A 1994 Kenworth W900L uses shade-shifting paint effects on the front fenders. *Not Too Blue* pulls a 1987 Dorsey reefer trailer. An owner–operator can individualize the W900 in a variety of ways, with choices for bumper, light panels, shiny quarter fenders, and a choice of horns and marker lights up top.

Opposite: A Kenworth T2000, part of the Prochnow Transport fleet, nicknamed *The White House*. This fleet favors Michelin tires because they are rugged, smooth riding, and reliable.

Below: A magnificent 42-wheel Michigan road train, a flatbed side-kit, and Kenworth T600 combo. The powerful graphics extend all the way down the sides of both trailers with lights on the fairing.

Retro Kenworth

Showtime evokes a 1949 Kenworth, '90s-style, from the custom made hood and period grille to strobes winking from headlights where turn signals reigned on the original. Even horn covers have been left out of the styling because there weren't any fifty years ago. Up front is a 1999 Kenworth W900L on a 350in wheelbase carrying a 165in x 102in custom sleeper. A 600hp Caterpillar engine cranked to 1000hp puts power to the road through an 18-speed Eaton transmission and 3.70 rears. The Texas square bumper has a beveled second tier light bar. The interior features shirred leather walls and UltraSuede accents.

Opposite: The flagship of Van Kampen Trucking, this is a futuristic, high-tech, and high-powered vehicle.

Right: At night the truck radiates lights. Even the chromed landing gear wears five purple lights in each brace, and neon below.

Left: A Kenworth T2000 grille. The sculpted aerodynamic lines are pleasing to the wallet as well as the eye by helping to eliminate air drag and promote better fuel mileage.

Opposite: This snappy red Kenworth T2000, one of Kenworth's aerodynamic models, is pulling a dry van in Chicago.

Below: A Kenworth T2000 at dusk just off Interstate 287, past the Toledo exit of Interstate 80. If that sounds confusing, it isn't. Truckers have been finding their way here for decades.

Above: Lots of shine and creatively placed lights beautify this venerable hauler, a 1978 Kenworth W900A on a 289in wheelbase (see also, right). This is a Louisiana "kitty" (nickname for Kenworth back in the Seventies). See also, opposite.

Opposite: A 1978 Kenworth W900A, *2 Legit 2 Quit*. The well-aged tractor is spiffed up with wire wheels and fancy custom mudflaps. Under the hood is a 400hp Big Cam Cummins with a 9-speed transmission and 3.70 rear ends.

Right: A restored 1960 Kenworth CJ925 and 1995 Freuhauf stainless steel van trailer (torsion suspension). The engine is a 262hp Cummins with 4 x 4 transmission. Riding on a 235in wheelbase, the tractor has a 36in bunk with crawl hole, the original "coffin sleeper."

Opposite: A Kenworth T600 combo. The sloped hood on this model Kenworth was a departure from the popular long square profile when introduced in the 80s. The T600's aerodynamic design promises and deliveres on fuel economy and performance.

Below: Florida trucker Jamie Hewett calls his 1999 Kenworth W900L Aerocab *Rooster Cruiser*. Hot flames lick the hood and fenders. It's got the "chicken hauler" look with heavy doses of lights, chrome, and custom accessories.

Above: *Feel the Passion* is a 2000 Kenworth W900L pulling a matching reefer. Created In 1990, the W900L a 130" BBC, long-nose conventional with extended hood, became an owner-operator favorite.

2001 W900

This 2001 Kenworth W900 day cab has power from a 550hp engine with 18-speed transmission and 3.70 rears. The tractor sits on a 225in wheelbase and there are 69 lights, all LEDS.

The truck pulls a 48ft reefer trailer hauling frozen food up and down the eastern seaboard. The two 120 gallon air tanks wear flamed end covers and all mudflaps are similarly painted.

Right: This Kenworth blazes with monochromatic flames and the cold sizzle of stainless steel on the deck, rear frame, boxes, visors, and suspension pieces.

Left: Owner, Blaise Verdino, foregoes the big bunk tractor, opting instead for a lighter-weight day cab.

Left: Winner by a nose, a curved one, that is, with a stylish grille that proclaims this is a Kenworth T2000, one of Kenworth's aerodynamic models.

Opposiite: There is no denying the kingly presence of a Kenworth W900 cruising the highway with a flatbed in tow.

Left: A rebuilt 1981 extended hood Kenworth W900A wears roof lights taken from a 1955 Kenworth, rechromed, and lenses replaced with old glass. Custom additions include chromed twin 6in stacks, aluminum deck plate steps, and painted fuel tanks banded in chrome. Gold anodized mesh brightens the air cleaners. The 60in factory bunk has a VIT interior package in dark red vinyl.

Right: Lights outlining the grille on an a classic owner-–operator enhanced Kenworth W900. The grill comes standard with three vertical struts; this one features seven. It is a popular option enhancement.

Below: A Kenworth W900L. The owner has optioned for an additional four struts on the grille to total seven.

Above: Etched metal on a W900. Even the stacks are curlicued straight to their tops.

Right: A Kenworth W900A with a bullhorn hood ornament and lights up each side of the grille, and under the grille and bumper.

Super-Customized W900A

King of the Road is one of the more creatively enhanced rigs on US highways. The 1980 Kenworth W900A on a 265in wheelbase is teamed with a 1980 Dorsey van set up as a mobile showroom. The rig is driven to truck shows and automotive racing events, selling souvenirs, gifts, novelties, flags, decals, teeshirts, and an arm's-length list of other goodies from the trailer inventory. Under the big K-whopper hood is a 400hp Cummins, 15-speed over-drive transmission, and 3.70 rears.

Left: This full-length mural on the front of the Dorsey trailer portrays a famous southern train called the General from the Civil War era. On the trailer's back doors, the mural shows the train's caboose with President Abe Lincoln and wife Mary waving from the platform.

Opposite: The large undies on the grille of King of the Road carry a variety of humorous sayings. Truckers bought them as bug screens and gifts. The more people laughed, the more they bought. They are now available in 150 designs and 40 colors.

Left: A classic long nose Kenworth W900B, though not as long a hood as the W900L (which is 10in longer), heads west on Interstate 80 pulling a spotless van trailer.

Opposite: A rare breed of trailer, this 48ft 2001 Western spread axle hopper flatbed can function like a side-kit or regular flatbed and as a hopper trailer. It is teamed with a 1996 Kenworth W900B. Power comes from a 500hp Caterpillar engine with 18-speed Fuller transmission and 3.70 rear ends. With the spread, total gross in western states can be 4000lbs higher, up to 84,000lbs, (or even higher with a special license). The way it works: the sides come up on hinges. Stakes, head, and back boards to finish the side-kit are carried up front. When the sides come up, certain floor pieces are removed to create a hopper. Left in, the trailer is a flatbed. The versatile hauler transports lumber, fertilizer, grain and steel, and salt in bulk or bags.

Above: A polished tri-axle dump truck, a W900, dressed with a stainless bowtie visor and lighted bumper.

Opposite and left: A Connecticut combo: Regis Beaudoin, BTC Inc., teams a 2000 Kenworth W900L with a 40ft frameless 2000 King Cobra end dump trailer. Six hundred Cummins horses strut under the hood, working through an 18-speed Eaton transmission and 3.55 rears. Wheelbase on the tractor is 255in.

Opposite: *Pumice Pearl*, a 2000 Kenworth W900B tri-axle dump truck that transports anything that can be fitted into the box bed.

Right: Exotic lighting adds a surreal look to this hard-working 2000 Kenworth W900B dump truck.

Opposite: Minnesota trucker Greg Brehmer owns and operates this 1999 Kenworth W900L on a 270in wheelbase. It is powered by a 600hp Cummins with 18-speed transmission and 3.55 rears. Chrome bumper is a bold and beautiful Texas square.

Right: This classic 1968 W900A Kenworth (glider kit) tri-axle dump truck has operated out of Sandusky, Ohio, for years shouldering loads of stone and asphalt. The owner Tom Brown speced it originally with an 8V71 Detroit (318hp) with 5-speed main and 3-speed auxiliary transmission and 4.33 rears. He ran it that way for one million miles and in 1975 installed an 8V92 Detroit (430hp) with an HP7P740 4-speed Allison Automatic transmission and 4.11 rears. In 1993 he changed it again, lengthening the frame, adding Peterbilt air-ride suspension, 3.70 rears, a Silver 92 Automatic and 4-speed auxiliary transmission plus two steerable front axles. The body throughout all these years has been the original 1968 Ravens dump body.

Cowboy Kenworth W900L

A 1996 Kenworth W900L on a 272in wheelbase is powered by a 500hp Cummins with 13-speed transmission and 3.90 rears. It uses a 2001 102 x 48ft East flatbed to haul pipe, coils, rods in various metals, as well as van freight. America's frontier days are recalled on the teal blue *Dream Catcher*. A dream catcher is painted on the back of the bunk and cut into the chrome bumper.

Above: The truck features contoured 7ft roof with 5in additional head room, skylights, and vented side windows. Styling reduces air drag and improves fuel effiency.

Below: When setting up a rig, the owner faces endless choices, from type of air cleaners, light bar packages, and engine and tanks, to chrome and stainless trims—targeting the finished product specifically for the type of haul.

Opposite: This Kenworth W900L day cab dump truck is overflowing with custom enhancements including stainless visor and cab lights, headlights in Double JJ brackets, and a hefty bumper punctuated with end lights. The cab is equally impressive, finished in a black and white checkerboard pattern.

Above: *Illusion*, a 1999 W900L. The truck is waiting to load mulch on top of a mountain in Lewiston, Idaho.

Left: The tractor is a 1998 W900L pulling a Michigan dump train, lit up like a movie marquee.

Opposite: *Mr Refuse*, a Kenworth T800 with a Leach Packer body combination.

Above: A 42-wheeled Michigan road train Kenworth W900 day cab with a light bar under the bumper, shiny dump boxes, and pinstriping.

Below: A 2002 blue Kenworth tri-axle with pinstriping and extra lights. Payloads are stone, sand, and salt.

Opposite: A T800 Kenworth dump truck powered with 550hp Caterpillar with 18-speed trannies behind them. The dump beds are by Williamson as are the dump pups pulled behind the truck. Pups have a hitch to pull an additional trailer. All pups run on super single tires. Sometimes the truck pulls one pup, as seen here, other times two. There are 5 axles on the truck, 4 on first pup, and 3 axles on the second. On each pup is a steerable lift axle and two on the truck. Overall weight with two dump bodies is 109,000lbs and with three, it is 129,000lbs.

Opposite: This ultra-sharp Kenworth, owned by Alpha Transport, Salt Lake City, Utah, carries a pair of tanks polished to blinding brilliance. Classified in western states as an LCV (long combo vehicle), it combines a straight truck plus full trailer, both placarded to signify that the commodity hauled is flammable.

Above and right: A giant tanker, Michigan style. This 2000 Kenworth W900L hosts a 550hp Caterpillar engine with 18-speed transmission on a 250in wheelbase. It pulls a 2000 model Bedard Asphalt Tank with 8 axles. Payload maxes out at 13,600 gallons. Every Michelin tire on this W900L combo has been lovingly hand-painted in patriotic colors.

Paradise is a W900L

To enjoy the artistry, color, and detail of *Almost Paradise* is nearly as satisfying as a cruise to a remote volcanic island in the South Pacific. The truck is flagship to Michigan-based "'77 Express." The tractor is a 1999 W900L Kenworth with a 500hp Detroit Series 60 pulling a 1996 Utility trailer. Tropically-themed murals depict a fantasy island surrounded by fish-filled waters.

Left: In the direct sunlight the murals leap to life. At night the area under the trailer is filled with neon light filtered through coconut-scented clouds drifting over a small wading pond. Under the fuel tanks, dolphins dance across stainless steel, backlit in neon. The front bumper features laser cut palm trees backlit in green and pink.

Opposite: On top of the trailer, directly above the painted volcano the owners rig a small "volcano" that spouts real fire.

PARADISE
'99 KENWORTH
W900L

• SOLD BY: MICHIGAN KENWORTH
GRAND RAPIDS, MI

• PAINT BY: SCOTTS SIGNS
GRANDVILLE, MI

• ENGINE: 500 DETROIT SERIES 60

• OWNED BY: MARV & BARB KNIGHT
77 EXPRESS AMBLE, MI

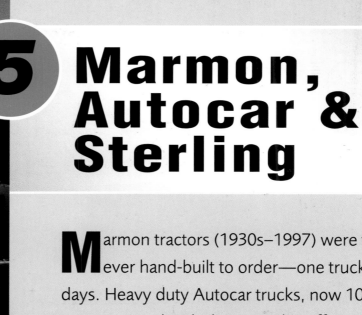

5 Marmon, Autocar & Sterling

Marmon tractors (1930s–1997) were the only trucks ever hand-built to order—one truck every 21 days. Heavy duty Autocar trucks, now 107 years old, are associated with dump trucks, off-road, and highway haulers. Sterling trucks offer custom-built tractors in three models: the A-Line, L-Line, and Acterra.

Left: In a convergence possibly more rare than a solar eclipse, three varying Marmon trucks from three different decades, '70s, '80s, and '90s, stand together at a truck show.

Opposite: Virgil Hawkins, a trucker for over fifty years, rebuilt his 1974 GHD Marmon with the help of son Jeff in their yard in Dunnellon, FL. He purchased it used in 1988 for $4500 and is the truck's fourth owner. Wheelbase on this blue Marmon is 255in. Engine is a 350hp Cummins (originally 290hp) with a Fuller 10-speed transmission and 3.91 rear ratio. It pulls a 48ft flatbed.

Above: The distinctive boxy silhouette of the Marmon 57P cannot be mistaken on the highway. The factory process in building this truck is legendary: every panel was cut and drilled, never stamped out. The cab doors were individually balanced and hung by hand for a perfect fit and seal. Full length piano-type hinges were used to prevent loosening. All insulation was cut individually.

Above: A 1986 Marmon transports dirt, stone, and sand.

Left: A Baltimore-based Marmon dump truck, added lights are included on the chrome bumper, chip guards, and dump bed.

Opposite: A rare Marmon 57P Premium Conventional. Factory specs included an all-aluminum cab, single piece hood, and polished aluminum grille and bumper. The engine was a Cummins Big Cam III, NTC 400@400 hp@2100 rpm, transmission an Eaton (Fuller) 13-speed with 4.11 Rockwell rears. Inside, the driver sat on an adjustable Bostrom air suspension seat. Accessories included dual chrome round air horns and an outside sun visor. Front suspension had 12,000 lb capacity, 38,000 on the rear suspension.

Marmon Model PH57

A 1987 Marmon model PH57 bought by the owners directly from the Texas factory—purchased new for $75,900. Wheelbase is 32in. Engine is a 400hp Caterpillar engine working through a Fuller 9-speed overdrive transmission, with a rear ratio of 3.73. It pulls a 48ft flat floor van for the transport of electronics and trade show displays.

Left: The owners built the bunk themselves to enhance their road life with everyday comforts. Features include an electric fireplace, rustic wood interior, microwave, refrigerator, TV, and satellite hookup.

Opposite: When older drivers see this truck, they tell the owner they wish they had one; others are curious about it because they've never seen one; and drivers who used to have a Marmon tell him they wished they had their old one back.

Below: On the side of this 1997 125DHR is a personal tribute to Marmon's employees. The owner had the idea after seeing one engineer break down and cry as he drove away with the last truck to be produced. The tribute reads "Extinction of excellence, the last MARMON, quality hand built, with sweat, tears, heartache, and PRIDE." The inscription also includes where the truck was built (Garland, Texas) and the date that it left the factory (2nd May 1997).

Above: There is no mistaking the big red plaque on the nose of this mighty Marmon. The owner replaced the original bumper with a stainless steel Texas style to make it look even more massive.

Opposite: This 1997 125DHR Marmon with a 250in wheelbase was purchased new from the factory for $87,000. It has been plying the highways every day to the present. The owner subsidizes his operation by selling advertising space on the 53ft 102in dry van.

Opposite: A 1966 Autocar Model A 10264 restored by Florida trucker Gina Kemner. The engine is a 350hp Cummins with 13-speed double overdrive transmission and 218in wheelbase. This workhorse has pulled a dump trailer (rocks, sand, asphalt), tanker (waste water), dry van (varied products including furniture, mattresses, sugar, pasta, tiles, canned goods), reefer (produce), and flatbeds (roof tiles, palm trees).

Below: This 1987 Autocar, *Legend*, is pulling a flatbed loaded with machinery. Drop deck and double-drop trailers have also been used on the trailer.

Left: More than fifty lights enhance this bobtail Model 7564T Autocar tractor. At night the lights create the illusion of a happy face, smiling.

Opposite: Two prize-winning triaxle dumps with steerable lift axles, restored by Maryland trucker Morris Neale, Dansville Hauling Corp., haul a variety of earth products in J & J 17ft dump bodies. On the left vehicle, only the spring hangers and steering wheel are original on this 1973 model Autocar. Power comes from a 400hp Cummins working through a 13-speed double-overdrive transmission and 44,000lb rear ratio. Right, this dark red 1979 Autocar is set up with a 290hp Big Cam 3 Cummins. They are part of a fleet of 25 dump trucks operating in the Washington, DC area.

Left: In Brooklyn, New York, Autocars and Macks have always been D&D Carting's trucks of choice. In 1988 these three trucks were D&D daily workhorses, photographed, along the East River under the famous Brooklyn Bridge. In the middle is *Iron Horse*, a powerful 1983 Autocar (see right and below). On the left is *Rolling Thunder*, a 1974 Mack DM 600 and *Hot Stuff* on the right, a 1972 Mack DM 600. All three have Leach packer bodies for hauling trash. The business is run today by the grandsons of Tony DiNardi who cofounded the company with Carlo DiCeglie in 1931.

Right: *Iron Horse* is a 1983 Autocar teamed with a Leach packer body for hauling trash. Under the hood is a 300hp Cummins, a 6 + 1 Spicer transmission with 55,000lb Rockwell rears, and rubber block suspension, not springs.

Custom Sterling LT9522

*T*ore Down is a 1999 Sterling LT9522 (L-line) delivering heavy machinery on a low boy trailer. The engine under the flamed hood is a 600hp Caterpillar engine. A 48in raised roof sleeper box and tag axle were added. Mudflaps on the back are cut out to say "Sterling." It hauls so heavy that it needs an added lift axle plus a gigantic ProTech headache rack and storage box to store the tie-down gear.

Left and above: An $8000 paint job: a riot of color from hood to fenders. This beauty shines with loads of chrome and stainless steel custom pieces

Opposite: The medium duty Sterling tandem axle AT9500 offers the strength and durability of a heavy truck in a compact size. Sterling trucks are custom-speced to the customer's needs, assuring the perfect combination of engine, transmission, rear axle ratio, and torque for the job.

6 Peterbilt

Peterbilt came to America's highways in 1939. Today Peterbilt offers a full line of beautifully designed, fine-crafted Class 6 to 8 trucks used in over-the-road hauling, construction, local delivery, and even logging. Popular with fleets and owner–operators alike, Peterbilt models feature a lightweight aluminum cab, a variety of suspension systems, and Unibilt® Cab Sleeper System packages that are available in lengths from 36in up to 70in, including the luxurious UltraSleeper.

Left: A 1999 Peterbilt 379 teamed with a Western walking floor trailer and tarped top. The payload is loaded from the top, then emptied through the rear doors by the motion of the floor.

Opposite and left: A 2001 Peterbilt 379, 600hp ISX Cummins with Eaton Fuller 18-speed transmission and 3.36 rear ratio. The 20in bumper is dressed with nine LED lights. Wheelbase is 310in. Trailer is a 2000 48ft Great Dane reefer temperature-controlled with a "King of the Road" ThermoKing unit. There are over 200 lights on this purple-hued rig and hideaway hub caps on the wheels. Inside: oak flooring and polished metal accents. An air tank assembly is custom made from a beer barrel for the truck's two sets of train horns.

Below: A Peterbilt 379 pulls a step deck trailer. The single toe pin centered in the bumper differentiates a 379 from the 359 Peterbilt.

Opposite: A 1982 Peterbilt 359 extended hood. The owner has stretched the frame and needle-nosed the hood, carving 12in from the grille. Preserving the traditional look, he added gold leaf flourishes and maximum stainless shine. Engine is an NTC 400hp Cummins with Fuller 146-8LL overdrive transmission and Eaton 3.55 rears. The hood operates hydraulically by switch and remote control. Note Harley-Davidson diamond-back headlights mounted in Double JJ brackets and chromed 8in straight pipes. Trailer is a 2000 Utility 48ft x 102in stainless steel dry van.

Below: Chevron DELO promotes its truck-friendly line of lubricants with this stately combo, a 2002 Peterbilt aerodynamic conventional 387 powered by a Cummins Signature 600 engine, pulling a 1998 SE Kentucky Manufacturing trailer. The contoured silhouette, distinctive grille fronting the sloped hood, and stylish headlight assembly give this truck a unique look.

Below: This cabover Peterbilt 282 pulls a drop deck trailer piled high with pipes. The shorter overall length model cabover is popular with haulers looking to increase their payloads by allowing for longer trailers. More hauling space equals higher revenues.

Oppposite: A 1982 Peterbilt extended hood. Cab is crowned with 13 visored bullet lights. Trailer is a 2000 Utility trailer stainless steel dry van with red fenders.

Left: The "Pete Classic" radiator cover is custom-made. This truck operates throughout Texas and New Mexico hauling nursery stock (trees) on a chrome-wheeled 48ft flatbed.

Below: An earlier variation of Thornhill's engine: chromed and stainless louvers dress the hood. Everything on the rear deck is custom aluminum diamond plate. No air horns; just classic bullet lights atop the cab.

Opposite: Tim Thornhill loves the classic styling and flat-topped sleeper of the 359 long hood Peterbilts. This 1986 model is the fifth 359 he has enhanced. The truck is never finished, ever evolving. An earlier variation is also seen here (see right), although this is the most recent. Lighted 22in stainless bumper bears laser-cut and back-lit words, "Trees Forever." Painted bands on air cleaners pick up the burgundy. Under the hood the 425hp Caterpillar is painted in the same colors as the truck.

Left: Under the needle-slim hood of this 1967 Peterbilt model 351 A is a 500+hp N14 Cummins with a 1700 series (high torque) 15-speed overdrive Eaton transmission. Wheelbase is 270in. Back fenders are diamond plate painted orange. It works every day, hauling heavy equipment on a flatbed or matching orange removable goose neck (RGN) 50 ton lowboy trailer.

Right: A Peterbilt 387 teamed with a matching van trailer. The aerodynamic conventional features a contoured roof cap that directs air around the trailer. Immediately recognizable is the sloped hood and sculpted fender design which optimizes airflow while maximizing visibility through the windshield.

Above: The first Peterbilt ever built back in 1939 was a log hauler. The make is still popular in logging camps and docks today, like this fiery metallic red daycab Peterbilt 378.

Opposite: The Peterbilt's air-suspension and air seat cushion the ride on the highway and off on the roads to logging sites.

Right: A 1967 Peterbilt needle nose model 351. The wheelbase extends a whopping 224in and carries a 145in custom sleeper. Murals on the truck are a tribute to the American farmer and to the John Deere tractors transported by this truck.

Opposite: This 1992 Peterbilt sustained critical fire damage in 1998. Pete Alan and his son rebuilt the truck, gave it a 425 B model engine, a 15-speed overdrive transmission and 3.55 rears, then put it to work pulling a dump bucket averaging a minimum of 2500 miles a week.

Right: On a farm in Yakima, Washington, this reefer combo was taking on a load of freshly picked ears of corn. The single stack red Peterbilt 359 is teamed here with a standard 48ft refrigerated trailer.

Opposite: A Champagne and Burgundy 2000 Peterbilt 379 pulling a 2000 Cottrell auto hauler trailer. Stainless panels on both tractor and trailer are studded with LED lights.

Left and below: This 2000 Peterbilt 379 is owned by Fairway Transit and driven by Kurt Krahn who helped design the dazzling graphics in reflective vinyl. The golden yellow is carried through in custom fender and tank covers. The steps are highly lacquered and there's an impressive line-up of lights.

Below and right: A 1998 Peterbilt 379 extended hood on a 276in wheelbase. A powerful 550hp Caterpillar beats beneath the hood, backed with an 18-speed and 3.26 rear ratio. These Florida truckers pull a flatbed, transporting steel and building products throughout the country. Fringed and beaded leather with conchos covers the shifter and southwest designs are etched into the base plate. Upholstery, graphics, and detailing—including etched windows—all evoke the spirit of the southwest.

Opposite: A 1993 Peterbilt 379 extended hood on a 308in wheel base with a 1998 Utility stainless steel spread axle reefer behind it.

2000 Model 379

An inky blue 2000 Model 379 Peterbilt "long hood" is outfitted with four 150 gallon tanks (on a 312in wheelbase) to fuel his weekly west-coast turnarounds. Fully fueled, the truck carries 300 gallons of fuel on each side of the stretched-wheelbase Peterbilt. Behind it is a 2002 48ft x 102in Great Dane refrigerated stainless steel trailer in which the owner, Linwood Hunt, transports beverages and food products. Maximum shine comes from polished aluminum wheels and stainless steel reefer.

Below and right: At current prices ($1.93/gallon/west coast), a fill-up of 600 gallons would cost over $1000. Check out the 18in stainless Texas-style bumper underscored with lights. The entire rig is dressed with 118 LED lights.

Opposite: This magnificent "Michigan train" measures about 89ft from its 22in front bumper to the rear. It is a 1990 Peterbilt 379 steel transporter powered by a 500hp Caterpillar 3406A. The transmission teams a Spicer main 60 with a 4-speed auxiliary.

Below: A quintessential owner–operator ride: long hood, custom bunk, and painted-to-match trailer. The 1989 Peterbilt 379 is teamed with a 425hp CAT and 18-speed tranny. Wheel base of 274in hosts an 84in custom bunk. The 1989 Utility spread axle reefer carries cheese and produce. The rig glitters at night with 185 lights overall.

Opposite: Flat top 1992 Peterbilt 379 is a combination of shiny stainless, Dupont Imron Red Metallic and Gloss Black, and close to 200 lights. A shiny chromed rooster perches on the hood. Engine is a 425hp Caterpillar 3406B with 15-speed transmission.

Above: A Peterbilt 379 lit by a setting sun pulls a tarped trailer. The discerning truck owner spices up the bumper by adding lights across the bottom. Note the lug nut covers on the steer tire rim.

Below: A Peterbilt 377 is a backdrop for hot air balloon vinyl graphics. It blazes at night with 325 lights. The long-hauling bobtail wears a custom 20in wraparound stainless steel bumper underlined with lights. Wheelbase is 335in, hosting a 166in sleeper. Engine is a 500hp Detroit with Eaton Autoshift transmission and 3.55 Rears.

Right: That's the window over the kitchen sink behind the stack. Custom stainless encloses headache racks and frames the rear entrance. Stained glass windows are on and above the door. Vinyl bras punch up color on fenders, tanks with blue, yellow, and magenta. The truck pulls a 1999 53ft Kentucky enclosed car trailer.

Opposite: *Shadow Dancer* grabs the eye with a high level of customization. The power unit is a 2000 Peterbilt 379 extended hood on a 325in wheelbase. It pulls a 1998 East drop deck curtain side trailer. Current graphics are reflective vinyl which gives the 78ft 6in long rig a dramatic and highly visible presence at night.

Below and right: This color-drenched combo features a 1986 Peterbilt 359 with a 140in custom bunk pulling a 53ft Kentucky trailer with lights everywhere. The riot of color halts at the hood, with the exception of a corner light at each end of the bumper, and the metal is kept clean. Few trailers are lucky enough to carry this level of custom graphics.

1997 Custom Peterbilt 379

A rolling piece of outrageously wonderful artwork, called *Kersplat* is a 1997 Peterbilt 379 on a 279in wheelbase that pulls cattle trailers and occasionally reefers. The 550hp Caterpillar engine is chromed. The interior features hardwood floor and oak cabinets. Intense "Peterson Purple" teams with shiny silver and blue rivers of molten color that dress everything from the cab to tanks, even to the frame and drive shaft.

Left and below: The beauty of this Peterbilt is in the details, like the "Kersplat" of color carried to the frame and tanks. SpectraLite neon lights underline the bunk.

Right: There are 576 louvers in the uniquely styled hood,13 lights across the cab top, and 65 lights overall including those on the chrome bumper. In an earlier version, a light bar of more conventional lights accented the bunk.

Above: This flatbed hauler is pulled by a Peterbilt 379. The side-kit on the trailer increases the flatbed's choice of payloads.

Right: A drop deck trailer pulled by a Peterbilt 359. Behind the truck is its pilot car which accompanies the truck, specially permitted because of its size, to check the route for bridge height, low wires, and other obstacles.

Opposite: This is a rebuilt 1991 Model 379 owned by Jerry Jeffries. Under the long red hood is a 3406 Caterpillar. Jeffries can't tell the horsepower, just that it was good enough to win the Palmdale Southwest National drags in its division. Wheelbase is 265in, twin stacks are 8in chrome. This truck is laden with custom stainless, chrome, and lights from Valley Chrome, Rig Skirts, and Peterson Lights.

Left: The 2001 Peterbilt 379 combines the passion of trucks and motorcycles held by its owner–driver Vladimir Bilik. Engine is a 600hp Caterpillar C-16 with 18-speed tranny and 3.36 rears. Fresh produce rides in a super-shiny 48ft stainless steel Great Dane spread axle with dual fuel tanks for the reefer unit. Check out the spare exterior styling, with suicide door, no cab lights, and chopped-low silhouette which help give *Peterod* its unique look.

Below: This 1992 aqua Peterbilt 379 is refreshing to look at. The owner–operator has extended the color to the rear, then accented the frame with chrome nut covers.

Opposite: An oldie but a definite goodie, the 1980 Peterbilt 359.

Opposite: Classically outfitted 1999 Hawaiian Orchid Peterbilt Model 379 on a 280in wheelbase. This hauler pulls a 1998 stainless steel Great Dane 48ft x 102in spread axle with a Phoenix Ultra Advantage cooling unit. Combo wears over 200 LED lights.

Right: The big log is no match for the Peterbilt 359, likely using a hefty dose of CAT power to transport its load.

Opposite: A Peterbilt 387. The uniquely shaped headlights, a big departure from the classic configuration, penetrate the storm and let the driver see farther down the road, helping to reduce fatigue.

Above and Right: The 1996 Peterbilt 379 extended hood is powered by a 500hp 3406E Caterpillar with 15-speed transmission, and 3.55 rears. Interior is a spectacular mix of stainless steel and lacquered rosewood. It transports fresh produce in a painted-to-match 1997 48ft Great Dane reefer dressed with a chromed-grille on the ThermoKing 300 unit. Not just your ordinary big red truck, this is a multi-award winning *Radiant Fire* Red Peterbilt featured on The Learning Channel's "Extreme Machines" television show.

Opposite: The tractor is a 1997 Peterbilt 379 extended hood riding on a 305in wheelbase and powered by a 550hp 3406E Caterpillar, Super 13 Speed Eaton, and 3.21 rear ratio. Bumper is 18in custom stainless steel. The 120in custom bunk was designed by the owner and his wife. Trailer is a 53ft spread axle US trailer auto transporter.

Opposite: The 1982 Peterbilt Model 359 is equipped with a 3406A Caterpiller 400hp plus-hp engine and 6in chrome straight pipes. Bunk is 36in. Typically 180 market size hogs or 38 head of cattle. ride in a 51ft x 102in 1996 double deck Eby Possum Belly trailer. Tractor and trailer sparkle at night with 225 LED lights.

Below: Sheep were being loaded onto this truck in the Sioux Falls, S.D. stockyards. The driver doubled as a shepherd, maneuvering his flock into the chute that channeled the animals into the trailer. Job done, his shepherd's crook was mounted on the outside of the trailer. You can see it there, just like crooks shepherds have used for thousands of years.

Left and above: A well-traveled combo: a 1963 Peterbilt model 351 and 1989 Great Dane reefer. The 400hp Cummins engine teams with an RT-1110 transmission and 3.70 ratio Rockwell rear ends. A unique bunk of the owner's own design sits on the 300in wheelbase. Note the length of the "needle nose" hood silhouette.

Opposite: A 2002 Peterbilt 379 extended hood teamed with a Silver Star livestock trailer. Among the custom touches on this tractor: "eyelashes" (visors) on the head-lights, a custom chrome bumper set with two framed lights, and a stainless drop visor.

359 Tractor and Reinke combo

Every inch of this outfit is painted and polished to perfection. The 1980 Peterbilt 359 is married to a 1985 63in flattop bunk and teamed with a 1999 46ft Reinke spread axle curtain van. The four million mile tractor and its companion curtain trailer are a showcase for creativity, from a composite grille incorporating Kenworth bars to chromed latches on the trailer doors.

Left: The truck's look evokes a low-riding custom machine. No grab handles. Hidden air lines (in the frame). Front end is dropped 3in, the mirrors 4in. Special plates hold mudflaps close to the ground. For balance, stacks extend to new heights, complementing the 14ft high trailer.

Opposite: The trailer's nose cone is front and center. Under the hood is a Big Cam 400 Cummins turned up to 500hp, paired with a 13-speed Fuller transmission. The bumper is a tapered 20in chrome slab with holeless bolt mount. Wheelbase is 250in.

Above: Like the fenders, the trailer frame is completely painted except for a narrow edge of polished aluminum all around.

Opposite: A 2000 Peterbilt 379 extended hood is a gorgeous combination of Mocha Pearl and Radiant Fire Red sitting on a 280in wheelbase. Sleeper is a 48in flat top. Under the hood is a powerful 600hp Caterpillar engine. The truck pulls reefers, transporting mainly food ingredients.

Above: This Peterbilt Model 379 backs its Great Dane reefer into a truckstop slot in California. Owner–operators like this one haul California's fresh produce to markets all over the country which service the grocery store chains.

Opposite: Indiana owner–operator Mike Floyd owns this 1998 light-sparked Mocha Pearl Peterbilt Model 379, seen here in the Boston harbor.

Below: A 1989 extended hood Peterbilt 379 on a 280in wheelbase. Note the unusual choice of color, the clean lines, sideways grille, and dearth of cab lights. This ride pulls a scrap wagon.

Left: A 1949 Peterbilt called *El Turbo*, with dual 6in straight chrome stacks, 310in wheel base and shiny 10ft sleeper, this Peterbilt is a head-turning legend on the West Coast. It is shown here with a 1983 Fontaine drop deck trailer. Power comes from a 400hp Cummins. Paint is Metallic Green Imron. Original wheels have been replaced with Alcoa aluminum all around. Note the chrome plated grille surrounds and hefty 24in front bumper with 30 LED lights. A total of 100 LEDs on the tractor turn up the brilliance at night. The diamond-embossed sleeper box is enclosed in polished stainless steel.

Right: An owner–operator Peterbilt 359 long hood on I-40 pulling a tarped flatbed heading west. The 359 Peterbilt has two toe pins in the front bumper.

Opposite: *Smokin' 99* is the name given to this smokin' rig scorched with hot blue flames. The all-black metallic combo 1999 Peterbilt 379 with 43ft 1999 Cornhusker hopper trailer primarily hauls feed ingredients.

Below: Tigator Trucking Service's distinctive long nosed Peterbilt 379s long hoods wearing a signature half tiger/half alligator.

Opposite: A twin-stacked Peterbilt 379 heavy hauler takes a curve in California. The drop deck trailer it is pulling takes on oversize equipment.

Right: An antique truck, this 1951 needle nose-style Peterbilt 350 is a 10-wheeler with separate pull trailer (normally 2 or 3 axles). It was licensed to pull as many as two added trailers with a gross weight of 120,000lbs. In this configuration it was dubbed a "Nevada Train" and truck licensed to haul on Nevada and Utah highways. Engine is a 400hp CAT. The headlights are stainless reproductions which won't rust like the originals.

Opposite: Riding its own ruby carpet (35 red lights) down the highway, this 2000 Peterbilt 379, owned by Curtis Christians, is decked out with 100 lights overall, styled in stainless and polished aluminum, flared with Harley Davidson accessories. Engine is a 600hp Caterpillar 3406E with Eaton Fuller 18-speed tranny and 3.36 rear ratio. The slab of chrome across the front is 21in with 4in boxed ends. It pulls a 2002 Great Dane refrigerated spread axle trailer.

Right: *Mis-Behavin'* is a 1953 Peterbilt 441. Paint shines in twelve shades of pearly blues, and there is an enchanting golden mermaid on the exterior back wall. Still pulling loads, it is powered by a 600hp CAT C-16 engine with a 5 x 4 transmission. Wheelbase is 300in with both cab and sleeper on a custom air-ride frame. Flat top look comes from chopping the sleeper, 3in from top and bottom. Freight rides in a 48 x 102in 2002 stainless Utility 3000R reefer with independent sliding spread axle and carries a T/K SB200 unit painted to match.

2002 Peterbilt 379

There's no such thing as too much shine on Pennsylvania owner–operator Rick Rollman's flamed and polished 2002 Peterbilt 379 extended hood powered by a 550hp Caterpillar engine. This is a working truck: pulling vans and reefer trailers throughout the east coast and Midwest.

The Pete has been meticulously transformed over a period of years, adding the newest clear-lens LED lights, custom fabricated accessories, even a purple and white tiled floor inside. All stainless work is by Pro-Fab Associates.

Above: Lift the hood and revel in wall-to-wall shine, from stainless steel spring covers to the heat shield and radiator reservoir tank, plus chromed shock, brake chambers, and alternator.

Left: From this angle it is possible to see how the flame motif unifies the truck's overall look. Stainless inserts dress the inside fenders and a ten-piece under hood accent kit adds shine to the underside of the hood.

Above: A 1999 Peterbilt 379 extended hood with a 120in custom sleeper. Both sides of the bunk wear these season-inspired murals by Scott Signs, Grand Rapids, Michigan. Here, on the driver's side, wolves stalk in a snowy landscape.

Opposite: A 1998 Peterbilt 379 extended hood and 1998 Utility spread-axle trailer. A prime example of a "rooster cruiser," the quintessential owner–operator's ride boils over with more than 200 LED lights from front to back and detailed with murals evoking the romance of the South Seas. The wheel holes are painted to match the truck. The truck hauls vegetables.

Below: On the passenger's side, the mural reflects summer's warmth. Deer romp beside a mountain stream. (See left also.)

Custom Pete

Spectacular horsepower. A 1990 Peterbilt 379 conventional hood tractor pulling a 1991 Great Dane refrigerated trailer. *Streaker* is a symphony in color, graphics, and customization. Engine is a 425hp Detroit with 15-speed OD. Wheelbase is 127in with a 63in custom stand-up sleeper. There are stampeding horses down the sides and the back doors are stainless steel, accented with red. In fact, just about everything on the truck is accented with red.

Right: In immaculate condition, the owner is continually adding creative new enhancements to the outfit to keep it fresh and new.

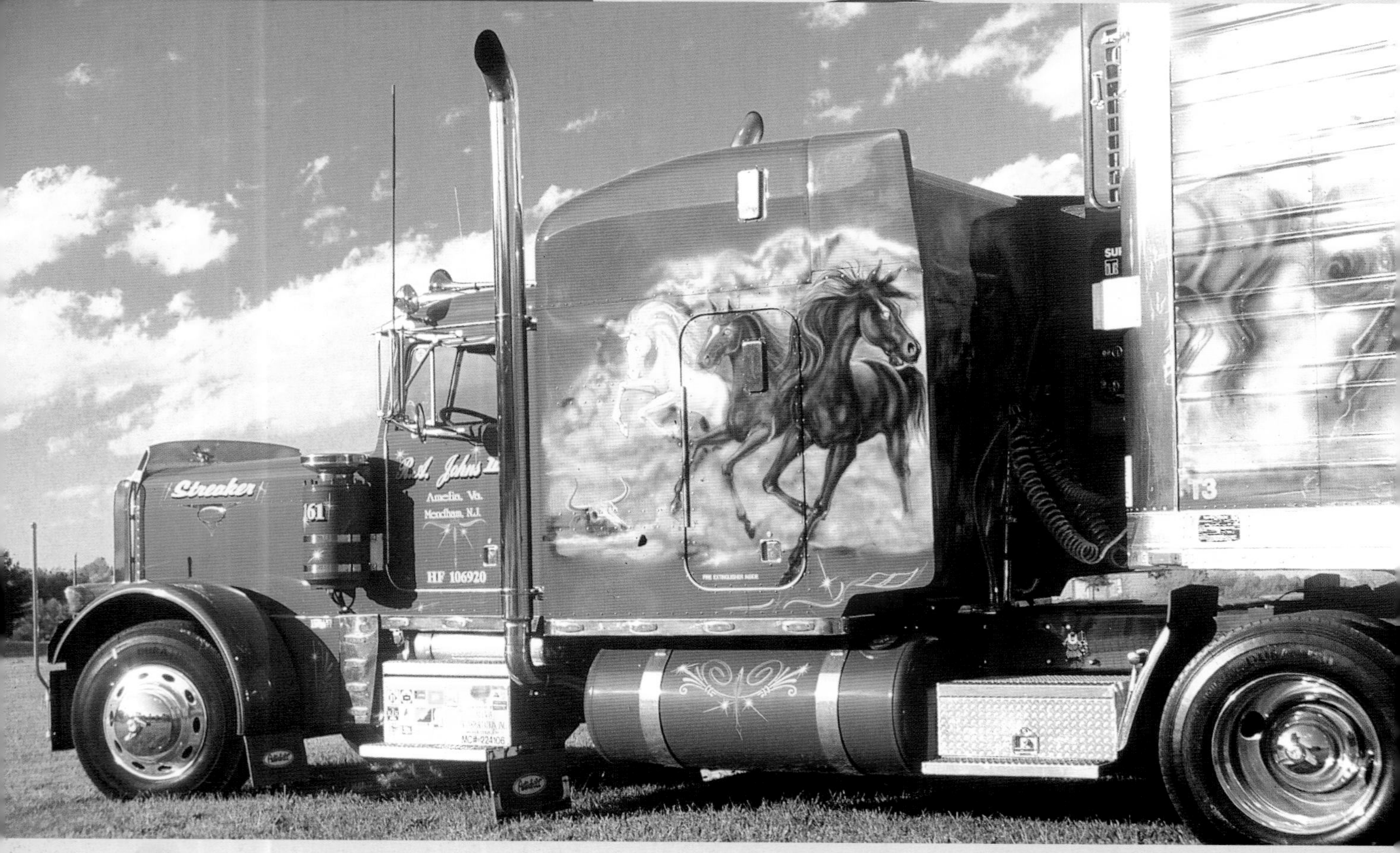
Streaker
161
Amelia, Va.
Mendham, N.J.
HF 106920
MC#224106
T3

Opposite: Much of the artwork is enhanced with gold leaf. All metal has been decorated with etched designs.

Below: Murals gallop across sleeper sides. On the back wall, long horned cattle churn up the dust.

Opposite: A tri-axle dump truck is a 2001 Peterbilt 379 speced with chrome straight pipes, 550hp Caterpillar 3406E engine and 18-speed transmission. The Summit body transports hot rocks (asphalt) The truck is decked out with tank covers, painted tank straps, and 270 LED lights. The back bumper/light bar alone wears 26 bezeled bulbs. The 22in box-style bumper carries nine lights.

Below: The Tri-State Commodities' distinctive orange and white rigs, in this case a Peterbilt 379 extended hood, transport feed commodities in hoppers, end dump, and dry bulk pneumatic trailers.

Below: Truck owner, Chris Jones, was one of the first truckers to use this look for fenders—a combination of polished aluminum and Indigo Blue paint. (See also, right.)

Right: This combination teams a 1986 extended hood Peterbilt 359 with a 40ft polished Cobra dump trailer with 10ft spread. Payload is sand and gravel. Under the hood is a twin turbo 475hp Cummins pushing 900hp. Transmission is an RTOO 14613 Roadranger with Eaton 3.55 rears.

Left: An end dump trailer fills from the top and empties from the back. Up front is an extended hood Peterbilt 359. The truck hauls mostly stone and sand.

Opposite: Red fenders, pinstripes, and stainless light bars on black make this rig a standout. The combo teams a 2004 Peterbilt with a 2003 Eby walking floor trailer. Payload is ear and seed corn.

Opposite: *Big Willy* is a 1990 Peterbilt 379 boasting a spectacular mix of style, lighting, and paint savvy. Under the hood is 460hp 3406B Caterpillar with 15-speed Fuller transmission, and 3.36 rear ratio. Lighting comes from 280 lights and 24 neon tubes. The 20in custom Texas bumper is outlined in 38 lights. Inside the massive bunk are full kitchen and bath.

Right: A 2000 Peterbilt 379, *Shadow Dancer* (as seen on page 269) shows the Peterbilt at night, its grille wreathed in neon light.

Right: This Peterbilt 379 extended hood pulls a 53ft dry van heading east across Utah's formidable mountains.

Below: The Peterbilt Model 387, with its characteristic sloped hood, shiny grille, distinctive bumper in Black Metallic paint with Galaxy Silver trim. Power choice is a 550 or 600hp CAT engine.

It's Showtime

Viper Red *It's Showtime* is a working truck used for rescue and heavy duty recovery of buses, trucks, airplanes, even fallen trees, throughout Illinois and southern Wisconsin. The 1999 Peterbilt 378 construction model's hefty engine is a 475hp Cummins with 13-speed transmission, and 44,000lb, 4.33 rears. Specialty features include a 70 ton Century rotator, 50,000lb towing underlift, two 60,000lb boom winches, 50,000lb deck winch, plus siren and train horn. It is loaded with custom stainless and chrome inside and out.

Above: Only with the hood down can this mural be seen, but the driver sees it all the time from behind the wheel.

Above: Dominant motif is flames—they appear all over, even in unexpected places like the bug shield, behind the visor, and inside the hood.

Below: En route to Salinas, California, this blue and white Peterbilt 376 pulls a wagon and pup filled with white onions. This two-axle tractor model is used for regional or local hauling.

Opposite: The noble nose on this Peterbilt 377 is artfully pinstriped, a motif repeated all over the tractor. The sharp-looking power unit pulls a dump trailer.

Left: A 1998 Peterbilt 379 tri-axle with an Alumitech 19ft body. Sixty lights add more razzle to this dazzling dump which transports concrete, dirt, and stone.

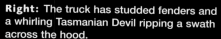

Right: The truck has studded fenders and a whirling Tasmanian Devil ripping a swath across the hood.

Below: A 2000 Peterbilt 379 tri-axle dump truck owned by Pennsylvania owner–operator Tony "Mountain Man" Rhoads. The rig is lit with 240 LEDs. Payloads are stone and sand transported in an 18ft aluminum Cobra body. Engine is a C12 430 CAT pushing 435hp.

Opposite: A tri-axle dump truck. This robust green Pete was ordered like this from the factory. Both visor and bumper were sand-blasted to give the paint a good grip. The painted bumper and visor matched to the body create a unique Peterbilt Model 379.

Opposite: A 2001 Peterbilt short nose 379 on a 347in wheelbase. This is a hard-working rig, carrying a Century 7035 boom on the back to tow trucks and buses. There are more than 300 LEDs plus auxiliary lighting, and 7in straight chrome stacks. Colors lean towards citrus hues, accented with colorful murals. Patriotic on the hood, the murals change tone on the tool boxes, showing an angel in the clouds watching over a painted rendition of the truck.

Right: Stone, sand, salt. Those are the primary payloads for this striking purple Peterbilt 379 tri-axle dump truck. The truck is customized with Harley-visored headlights and extra lights on the bumper. This truck works every day, in and out of quarries and construction sites.

Below: The *Green Hornet*, a 1967 model 358 A, needle nose tilt Peterbilt tractor converted into a showy ten-wheel dump truck. The "A" in the model means the frame is aluminum. The 13in bumper is chrome. Under the hood is a 1989 Cummins 350hp Recon, a small cam pumped up to a tad over factory specs, which replaced the factory-installed FFC 290 in 1997. The fifth wheel was replaced by a "scissor jack" to raise the rock box (tub). Among its payloads: scrap steel, rock, sand, dirt, cold patch for potholes, and broken cement. Now it's shown at regional trucking events.

Opposite: A 1998 Peterbilt 379 takes on a load of stone in the tri-axle's 17ft box. Power comes from a 430hp C12 Caterpillar engine.

Opposite: *Outrageous Transport* is an apt name for this purple 2002 Peterbilt 379 dump truck. Power comes from a 550hp Caterpillar 3406E teamed with an 18-speed Eaton transmission. Up front is a 23-light-enhanced 18in chrome box end bumper. The hand-crafted custom rear bumper features six Double JJ blinker light bars. Wheelbase is 265in. The owners added 150 lights and designed all the custom pieces. The 18.5ft Bibeau steel "dump bucket" carries mostly general aggregate and works in mason supply yards and on construction sites.

Right: A 1998 Peterbilt 379 tri-axle dump truck, hauling stone and asphalt in eastern Pennsylvania. Hot pink graphics stand out against the Bimini Blue base paint.

Left: A Peterbilt 377 pulling a hopper trailer filled with grain. The load will be leaving the trailer through hoppers in the bottom of the box.

Opposite: Murals with a Native American theme highlight this Flame Red 2001 Peterbilt 379 tri-axle dump truck. Under the long red hood is a 550hp Caterpillar engine with 18-speed tranny and 4.33 rears. The truck is dazzled with 205 lights, including those on the 18in Texas square bumper. An R & S aluminum body transports stone, sand, and top soil.

Opposite: This red 1990 Peterbilt Model 379 short hood, teamed here with a 1990 Cobra 30ft box (31ft frame) tri-axle dump trailer, is one of a fleet of end dumps and pneumatic dry bulk tankers.

Right: This 1988 Model 377 Peterbilt with a Timpte Super Hopper trailer that is being loaded through the open top. The versatile hopper can carry grain, meal seed, limestone—almost anything that's dry and will flow out through hoppers in the bottom of the trailer.

Peterbilt Fleet

An all-Peterbilt fleet owned by Tom Eilen & Sons and all the trucks were designed by the sons. All three rigs transport salt in winter, and in warmer months, sand, gravel, decorative rock, plus asphalt. They pull a variety of trailers, from liquid fertilizer tanks to flatbeds and vans.

Below: *Nitro Bucket*—a 2003 Peterbilt 379 extended hood tri-axle on a 300in wheelbase. It gets its power from a C12 Caterpillar 455hp engine. Transmission is an Allison Automatic with a 4.10 rear ratio. Dump box is a 21ft Cobra.

Below left: *Let's Ride* is a 2003 Peterbilt 379 extended hood with a 48in flat top bunk. A powerhouse 550hp C15 Caterpillar crouches under the hood. Transmission is 18-speed with a 3.55 rear ratio. Wheelbase is 270in. The equally striking tri-axle end dump trailer is a 2003 Mac 34ft box on a 35ft frame. All lights on this rig are LEDS under clear white lenses.

Left: A 2003 Peterbilt 379 extended hood with 36in flat top. Emblazoned across the back is the motto, *Drive to Live, Live to Ride*. Engine is a 550hp C15 Caterpillar, with 18-speed transmission and 3.55 rears. Wheelbase is 270in.

Opposite: A strikingly striped Peterbilt 379 short hood pulling a pneumatic dry bulk tanker.

Below: A two-tone Peterbilt 379. This shiny rig transports flammable products.

Opposite: This rig is a 359 pulling a pair of bulk tankers out of Ontario, California.

Below: A 1988 Peterbilt 377 and highly polished double stainless tanks.

Left: This is a 1995 Peterbilt 379 multi-axle combination. Engine is a 500hp Cummins. Hitchcock's rigs can be 70–75ft long overall. Net weight of product in the tanks can go as high as 104,000lbs. Gross weight on these rides can top 156,400lbs.

Opposite: This is a 1996 Peterbilt 379 pulling a 32-wheel tanker (a total of 42 wheels). Tanks, baffled and unbaffled, haul liquid fertilizer, calcium chloride, and feed products. Under the hood, a 550hp CAT with 18-speed transmission and 3.90 rears. Using seven- and eight-axle trailers, there's a lot of rubber and aluminum riding under the truck.

Opposite: This 1985 Peterbilt cabover 362 comes equipped with an electronic automatic transmission. The 200in wheelbase hosted a 110in sleeper. Power came from a 400hp 3406B Caterpillar engine. The truck hauls liquid soap.

Right: A dramatic tanker combo, a 1992 Peterbilt 379 and rebuilt 1978 stainless steel 42-foot Heil single compartment tanker, makes bold use of color and lights. The flat top sleeper is preferable for easy maneuvering. The combo is called, *Liquid Chicken*, a name inspired by the payload of rendered (mostly chicken) nonfood-grade fats.

7 Mack

The sturdy, hard-working Mack truck has become part of America's lexicon and the Mack bulldog logo has come to represent tenacity, strength, and toughness. The one hundred and four year old company began in Brooklyn, New York at the turn of the 20th Century and, while it moved to Allentown, PA in 1906, the ties to Mack are strong, as seen from the many R models in service throughout the "Big Apple."

Left: This Mack CH600 pulls a van trailer. Bulk or freight hauling, this Mack could do it all. Its standard axle-back configuration offers a tight turning radius and excellent weight distribution.

Below: A 1989 Mack model RW613 Mack Superliner II on a 270in wheelbase. Under the hood is a powerful E-6 350 engine with RTLO 18918B transmission (18-speed). Original bunk is a 42in Able flat top style. The 2003 Great Dane 53ft spread-axle trailer transports machinery, trade shows, and air freight. This Mack has over 100 lights, including 22 bulbs under the trailer.

Opposite: This striking Mack CH600 takes its image seriously. The CH-Series is a high performance conventional model with a shorter hood than the CL-Series and is well-suited for bulk hauling.

Opposite: A Red Mack Super-Liner conventional. Power comes from a 500hp V8 engine backed up with a 9-speed transmission and 4.17 ratio rears. Front suspension is 3-leaf tapered spring, 12,000lb rated front axle. Wheelbase is 260in. Trailer is a 48ft 1986 Utility reefer dressed with lots of chrome and stainless.

Right: A Dark Metallic Blue Super-Liner Mack is a "half-breed" because it uses a Cummins engine instead of a Mack model. This heavy-duty hauler has a tilting fiberglass hood and an air-suspended galvanized steel cab. The squared silhouette evokes memories of the hardworking R model.

Left: Intermodal containers like the one this Mack CH600 is pulling, are lifted off ships, and placed onto wheeled trailer frames for transport.

Above: A Mack Vision is a premium long-haul highway truck. This model has become popular for its roomy, air-suspended cab and sleeper combinations, available in 48in flat top, 56in flat top, 60in mid-rise and 70in mid-rise configurations.

Opposite: A CH600 model Mack, its sleek hood and sloped windshield, pointing to its Mack lineage.

Opposite: A CH600 Mack, bumper, and wheels shined to the max. A fleet truck, this CH600 is known for its powerful, yet lighter weight Mack E7 engine (600-800lbs less than its bigger competition) which means the truck hauls more frieight. With its sloped, medium nose it can pull a longer trailer and host a bigger sleeper.

Right: A CH600 Mack with a van trailer. For the long hauler, the interior on this model is ideal: comfortable, handsomely appointed, with switches and gauges within easy reach, the steering wheel adjustable for driver comfort, and the dash well-lit.

DM600 Mack

olling Thunder is a 1974 Mack DM 600 and *Hot Stuff* is a 71 Mack, same model. Both carry 25cu. yd Leach packer bodies. They are speced with 237hp Mack engines. The 1974 truck teams with a 5-speed transmission and 44,000lb rears. The 1971 has a 5-speed overdrive with 58,000lb rear ends. These trucks have been picking up trash off the streets of the Big Apple since 1931. In those days a horse and wooden cart did the job. Today it's diesel horses and specialized metal "wagons."

Left: The truck's owners are D&D Carting in Brooklyn, New York. J. DiNardi's grandsons, Anthony Jr. and Jack run it and have put a boldly colored, heavily shined face on their 10-truck fleet of Macks and Autocars. They specialize in transporting industrial waste.

Opposite: This Mack CH600 powers an intermodal container. The CH's aerodynamic design, lightweight components, and advanced electronics give it the versatility for both standard and off-highway applications

Right: A red CH600 model Mack was heading for the Canadian border. The tarp on the side of the trailer indicates this is likely to be a hopper trailer that loads from the top and empties from chutes (hoppers) in the bottom of the trailer.

Below: This Mack is a CH600 model, a dependable tractor, with a set-back axle to give it good maneuverability and a sloped hood for excellent visibility.

Below: A Mack CH600 day cab. A clear line of vision from the sweeping windshield and the 45-degree wheel cuts make the Mack CH600 well-suited to maneuver its payload into any loading dock, alley, or tight spot. Engine diagnostics can be performed with a hand-held Pro-Link® computer, a boon for fleet maintenance.

Above: A Mack Vision pulling a tanker. The standard axle-back configuration has an axle to back of cab dimension of 63in and that length translates into a tight turning radius. An optional axle-forward version measures 82in.

Opposite: Prospective truck buyers come to truck shows like the Mid-America Trucking Show to shop for new rides, like this Mack CH600.

Left: A restored 1963 Mack B61. The B series was sold between 1953 and 1966, and sold more than 47,000 units. Engine is the original E673 with an (estimated) 178hp. The wheelbase has been stretched, the original suspension removed and replaced with air-ride.

Below: Fully loaded flatbed gets pulled up a mountain in Scranton, Penna. by a CH600 model Mack.

Opposite: Drag-racing Mack R models wearing the signature green and red coloration of New York City trash haulers, enjoy a day at the US Diesel Truckin' Nationals, held annually since the 1970s at Englishtown Raceway Park in New Jersey.

Below: Take a close-up look at the "M" grille that instantly identifies the Mack Vision. The sleek aerodynamic lines are a signature of this popular Mack model.

Above: Great looking CH600 day cab Mack teams up with a refrigerated trailer for regional hauling.

Opposite: Cross-country and line-haul drivers appreciate the comfort and styling of the Mack Vision series, available with 70in mid-roof sleepers and 113in BBC. Well-designed and loaded with amenities like fully reclining seats. Engines are Mack-made with a choice of automatic and manual transmissions.

Opposite: Pioneer Carting & Recycling, Manhattan, Ny. owned this Mack RB600 and painted Leach Packer. The murals on both sides show the days of stagecoaches and pioneers. John Florio and Stephen Florio, Jr. designed the truck, heavy with lights, pinstriping, and chrome. The axle-back design of the Mack RB600 truck shortens the wheelbase and decreases its turning radius, making short work of tight spots on the construction site or in landfills. It also permits increased weight transfer for maximum payload.

Right: There is a galaxy of lights on the front end and a pinstriped chrome bumper (see left also).

Opposite: Vision, is an air-suspended cab and sleeper. Dash is fully electronic wraparound design, and sleeper cabs are available in three different configurations as well as engine/transmission choices. Sleeper choices are 48in flat top, 56in flat top, and 70in mid-rise.

Above: This Coney Island Rubbish Removal, Inc.'s green R model Mack is spiced with colorful paint and lots of chrome. The "Joker" face on the truck was a tribute to the grand dame of amusement parks, Steeplechase, on Coney Island in New York City. The owner has a full back tatoo of the Mack.

Left: Custom chrome bumper on this Pennsylvania Mack CL600 dump truck is a beauty, underscored with lights. The CL series accommodates the most powerful engines and is available in a variety of configurations for highway and off-road uses.

The Mack Bulldog

Mack owners have a good time customizing their Macks through the use of murals, lights, chrome, and stainless steel. One cool clique of Mack buffs enjoy outfitting the patented bulldog hood ornament in all manner of ensembles: the dog's collar is colored, and sunglasses and tiny clothes are added. All in good fun.

The bulldog ornament is a world-famous trademark that has come to represent anything rugged, tenacious, and determined, a reputation that came from the AC Model Mack's performance in World War I. The truck became known as the "Bulldog Mack," for its toughness and dependability. The now famous hood ornament was designed and patented in 1932 by Mack Chief Engineer Alfred F. Masury and has perched atop Mack radiators ever since. The story is that Masury carved the original bulldog from soap with a pen knife, giving it a chunky angular look and aggressive pose that captured its truck namesake.

Below: Nothing like a pair of sharp black shades to add swagger to a Mack bulldog.

Above: If the Blues Brothers were looking for a mascot, here it is.

Right: Señor Bulldog—very cute and typical of the creative ensembles foisted on these willing chromed pups.

Opposite: A CH600 Mack. Painter is Butch Yocum. Unique in an all-Mack fleet of 147 trucks, this Mack glider kit was built to honor 9/11 victims, in particular the memory of the owner's good friend Bruce Reynolds, a New York Port Authority officer killed that day.

Below: A Mack CH600 long nose conventional, white overall, with purple accents and small turbo wings on the fenders. The white bumper and fairings help make the rig look longer. This versatile truck can handle both highway and logging camp sites with ease.

Below: This Mack R model and Fruehauf bucket combo hauls coal, stone, and gravel. The R series conventional was introduced in 1965 and discontinued in 1987.

Opposite: The R model Mack tri-axle dump truck, this one a 2001 model.

Left: Sand, gravel, and dirt ride in the back of this 2004 R model Mack tri-axle dump truck. The box is a J-Craft end dump. Powering this Minnesota-based truck is a 400hp Mack engine with a 6-speed transmission. The chrome bumper adds extra sparkle.

Right: A Mack Vision fleet tractor pulls a painted tanker. The tractor's wraparound windshield and sloped hood give the driver exceptional visibility which translates into a big safety bonus. Powered by the Mack E-Tech® engine with V-MAC® electro nics, the combination provides fleet managers and owner–operators with the efficiency and vital information they need to squeeze more productivity out of a rig.

Left: A Mack CH600 day cab shouldering a tanker load of asphalt. The CH series day cab, with its axle-back configuration and high-horsepower category makes it a solid choice for a variety of hauling applications, like bulk-haul, van, and flatbed.

Opposite: The R model was introduced in 1965 and more than 200,000 have been sold in their 22 years.

Below: Straight tank trucks are frequently teamed up with a Mack CH600, a truck model known for its solid performance, maximum maneuverability, and flexibility to accommodate customization requests for specialized hauling.

8 Western Star

Western Star Trucks, established in 1967, offers an estimated 8,000 options for its vehicles including engine, transmission, axle, and chassis combinations. The trucks are known for their rugged construction and are popular with owner–operators as well as off-road operations in construction, logging, mining, and oil field services.

Left: *Autumn Run*, a 1998 Western Star Constellation on a 280in wheelbase with 92in custom sleeper. Engine is a 550hp Caterpillar with 18-speed Eaton tranny and 3.73 rears. The trailer is a 48ft 2000 Dorsey stainless steel spread-axle dry van. The truck wears over 200 LED lights, plus stainless steel and polished aluminum pieces.

Opposite: This is a 1995 Western Star 4964F with 54in sleeper. Powertrain starts with a 435hp 3406 CAT engine with Super 10 transmission and 3.73 rears. Rubber is 11R24.5 all around. A shorter wheelbase and small sleeper contribute to a lighter tare weight of 29,000lbs which translates into a bigger payload. Note how the accent colors are picked up in the headache rack and on the trailer frame. (Headache rack: flatbedders use them to prevent loads from crashing through the back of the tractor in case of an accident, thereby preventing a "headache.")

Right: The smaller sleeper still gives the look of a "big truck" but allows for a shorter, 235in, wheelbase which, combined with the shorter hood, contributes to the maneuverability of this rig. Custom touches include the light bar below the bumper and polished aluminum wheels.

Custom 1998 Constellation

A 1998 Western Star *Constellation*. The bawdy jester on the hood sets the tone for purple roof equipment. Engine is a 500hp Detroit series 60 with 15-speed transmission. Note the stained glass window at the front of the 150in sleeper box. Lights are everywhere, a total of 1142, mostly LED but also neon and fiber optics. It helps to have a 7000 Kubota generator on board. Wheelbase on this beauty is 525in.

Below: Back wall of the sleeper is custom stainless as is the deck. From this angle you get a good idea of where some those 1142 lights are, including the awesome back light bar, light-encrusted fenders, and long lines of lights on the bunk.

Opposite: Murals depict the French quarter and the famous Krewes parades. Base paint is a custom mixed White pearl. Mardi Gras colors of green, gold, and purple can be found in the neon and LED lights, and accessories inside and out.

Below: Closeup look at a Western Star 4964F and flat top 54in sleeper teamed up with a refrigerated trailer. The sloped tilt hood improves visibility and driver safety. A torsion spring tilt-assist makes it a whole lot easier for the driver to raise and lower the hood.

Above: A twin stack Western Star 4964 Constellation strolls down the highway with a flatbed in need of a load. Those poles mounted on each side of the bumper are guides to help the driver know where the corner of the bumper is. They are particularly helpful to drivers of long-hood conventionals. Although some truckers refer to them as "rookie rods," experienced drivers, who own long hood trucks like these, favor their use. The tops of the rods can be lighted and decorated.

Opposite: This Western Star 5964 pulls an oversize load on a flatbed.

Below: A twin-stack model 4964F. A unique severe service radiator mounting system isolates this component from road shock. Solid steel cabs are welded instead of riveted, dashboards are built with a strong metal substructure, and there is higher ground clearance for elevated positioning of fuel tanks and crossover lines.

Opposite: A 1987 Western Star 4964 with a Star Light sleeper is substantially lighter (the result of aluminum skins bonded to a polypropylene honeycomb core) resulting in increased payload carrying capability. The tractor is teamed with refrigerated trailer, lavished with 80 lights and custom enhancements. A custom light bar is mounted under the bumper.

Left: A High top Western Star Constellation pulls a dry van. The large windshield offers improved visibility, five-arm west coast-style mirrors. The sleepers on this model are available in five sizes, 42 to 72in, with high and low roof styles. The owner–operator has carried through their colors on tanks, trailer, and landing gear.

Opposite: It takes a tough truck like the Western Star 4864 to pull a 34-wheel tank. The truck frame rails are drilled, not punched, and tubular crossmembers offer strength, greater frame durability, and directional stability.

Below: A 1987 Western Star with flat top sleeper, pulling a 1991 48ft Great Dane reefer. Engine is a 400hp Cummins with 15-speed Fuller transmission and 3.55 rears. Wheelbase is 275in. Enhancing this seasoned hauler are 140 lights and 5in chrome straight pipes.

4964EX Constellation

This 2000 Western Star Constellation 4964EX looks too good to be hauling out of quarries. The stainless-enhanced all-steel day cab sits on a 270in wheel base.

The tractor is powered by a Signature 600hp Cummins, 18-speed Eaton, and 3.90 Eaton rears. The end dump trailer is a 2001 30ft Hill air-ride tri-axle that transports sand, gravel, concrete, rock, and dirt.

Left and right: Brightening construction sites throughout the New York City's five boroughs, this working truck glows with 262 clear-lensed LEDs.

Below: Silver letters outlined in pink spell out "Mama's Wild Child" on the hood and "Quick Turnover" on the bug deflector. The chromed bumper is enhanced with a polished aluminum light bar.

Right: A Red Metallic 1987 Western Star. The cab sits on a 230in wheelbase, every inch of it painted and pinstriped, set off with two polished aluminum tanks. A 425hp CAT engine drives through a 15-speed double overdrive transmission. Rears are 44,000 Rockwells with a 4.11 ratio. Payloads ride in a Hill dump trailer, the 26ft tub carried on a 28ft frame.

Index

Autocar dump trucks
    234–5
Autocar *Legend*, 1987 233
Autocar Model 7564T 234
Autocar Model A 10264, 1996
    232–3
Autocar trash trucks 236–7

Caterpillar 50, 60, 74, 86–7,
    108–9, 111, 112–13, 158–9,
    160–1, 165, 172, 176, 178–9,
    180, 184, 202–3, 218, 228, 238,
    249, 258, 262–3, 265, 270, 273,
    275, 280, 283, 285, 291, 299,
    301, 302, 311, 317, 318, 326,
    330, 333, 334, 338–9, 344, 347,
    383, 385, 396
Cummins 52–3, 54–5, 80, 84–5,
    98–9, 109, 116–17, 120–1, 122,
    137, 146, 152–3, 166, 188–9,
    200, 204–5, 208–9, 210, 224–5,
    226–7, 233, 234, 237, 243,
    244–5, 250, 286, 288–9, 312,
    320, 344, 353, 392, 394

Detroit 50, 62–3, 72–3, 74, 83,
    84–5, 89, 95, 164–5, 209, 220,
    266, 306, 386
Dorsey 109, 142, 176

Eaton 54–5, 62–3, 72–3, 95,
    120–1, 164–5, 165

Freightliner cabover 42, 54–5, 84,
    88–9
Freightliner Century CS/T 58–9,
    59, 64, 64–5, 66, 66–7, 68, 70,
    70–1, 74, 74–5
Freightliner Classic XL 44, 44–5,
    45, 48–9, 82–3, 89
    132, 1986 60
    132, 1995 86–7
    132, 1996 72–3
    132, 2001 42, 52
    2000 76, 76–7
    Limited edition, 2001 62–3
Freightliner Columbia 50, 51, 56,
    56–7, 57, 64
Freightliner dump truck 76–7, 80–1
Freightliner FLD 120 86, 89, 46–7,
    47, 48, 49, 54, 68–9, 78, 78–9,
    80, 84–5
Fruehauf 159, 189, 376

Great Dane 52–3, 95, 114–15,
    120–1, 122, 350, 392–3

International 4070 B Transfer II
    109

International 9000 series 122–3,
    130
International 9100 128, 130–1
International 9200*i* 105
International 9900 130–1
International 9900*i* 110–11, 125
International 9900*ix* 105
International cabover 107, 124–5
International dump truck 128–9
International Eagle 9300 104–5,
    106, 114, 115, 118–19, 119, 122
    1982 120–1
    1996 124
    1998 106–7, 116–17
    1999 108–9
International Eagle 9400 112–13,
    115, 116, 122–3, 128–9
International Emoryville A model,
    1965 111

Kenworth cabover 159
Kenworth CJ925 189
Kenworth K100 154
Kenworth Limited Edition 159
Kenworth T600 133, 138–9, 145,
    146–7, 183, 190
Kenworth T800 136–7, 151, 155,
    214–15, 216–17
Kenworth T2000 133, 138, 148–9,

168, 168–9, 182–3, 186–7, 194
Kenworth tankers 218–19
Kenworth tri-axle, 2002 216
Kenworth V100E 159
Kenworth W900 133, 133–4,
    144–5, 163, 174, 192, 194–5,
    198, 199, 205, 215
Kenworth W900A 158–9, 170,
    188–9, 196–7, 199, 200–1
Kenworth W900B 135, 162–3,
    174–5, 202, 202–3
    1983 170–1
    1984 150–1
    1991 170
    1994 134–5
    2000 206–7
    Aerodyne 151
Kenworth W900L 140–1, 198,
    212–13
    1992 180
    1994 180–1
    1996 210–11
    1997 164–5, 172–3
    1998 142–3, 152–3, 213
    1999 149, 156–7, 165, 166,
        176, 184–5, 213, 220–1
    2000 178–9190, 204–5, 218
    2000 Aerocab 137
    2003 160–1

Mack B61, 1963 365
Mack Bulldog 372–3
Mack CH600 348–9, 350–1, 354,
   354–5, 356–7, 360–3, 365, 366,
   374–5, 380
      Day cab 363, 380
Mack CL600 371
Mack Coney Island Rubbish
   Removal Inc. 371
Mack DM600 236–7, 358–9
Mack R series 364–5, 376, 376–7,
   378–9, 380–1
Mack RB600 368–9
Mack Super-liner 352–3
Mack Super-liner II RW613, 1989
   350
Mack Vision 354, 363, 366,
   366–7, 370–1, 379
Marmon 222–3, 226
Marmon 125DHR, 1997 230–1
Marmon 57P 225
Marmon 57 Premium Conventional
   226–7
Marmon dump truck 226
Marmon GHD, 1974 224–5
Marmon PH57, 1987 228–9

Peterbilt 254–5, 294, 314–15
Peterbilt 282 cabover 246
Peterbilt 350, 1951 299
Peterbilt 351 253, 286
Peterbilt 351 A, 1967 250
Peterbilt 358 A, 1967 330
Peterbilt 359 255, 273, 279,
   294–5, 314, 342–3
      1980 276–7
      1982 244–5, 284–5

      1985 288–9
      1986 248–9, 269, 312–13
Peterbilt 362, 1985 346–7
Peterbilt 376 322
Peterbilt 377 266–7, 322–3, 334,
   337, 343
Peterbilt 378 252–3, 320–1
Peterbilt 379 265, 273, 297,
   298–9, 311, 318–19, 326–7, 329,
   340–1
      1989 263, 293
      1990 262–3, 306–9, 316–17,
      334–7
      1991 272–3
      1992 263–4, 276, 347
      1995 344
      1996 280, 344–5
      1997 270–1, 282–3
      1998 258, 292–3, 304–5,
      324–5, 330–1, 333
      1999 240–1, 278–9, 296–7,
      304
      2000 256–7, 260–1, 268–9,
      290–1, 300–1, 317, 326
      2001 242–3, 274–5, 310–11,
      328–9, 334–5
      2002 286–7, 302–3, 332–3
      2003 338–9
Peterbilt 387 245, 250–1, 280–1,
   318
Peterbilt 395 174
Peterbilt 441, 1953 301
Peterbilt dump trucks 310–15,
   322–7, 329–35, 334–7, 338
Peterbilt extended hood 246–7,
   258–9, 268–9, 280, 293, 318–19,
   338–9

Sterling LT9522 238–9

Trailers
   Auto-hauler 48–9, 146–7, 256–7,
      282–3
   Bucket 376
   Bulk 82–3, 84–5
   Drop deck 108–9, 246, 268–9,
      298–9, 273
   Dry box 66
   Field 78–9, 124–5
   Flatbed 44–5, 46, 78, 84–5, 96,
      114, 116, 122–3, 125, 132–3,
      144–5, 183, 194–5, 202–3,
      210–11, 233, 258, 273, 294–5,
      365, 384–5, 388–9
   Hopper 296–7, 334, 337, 361
   Intermodal container 64–5, 93,
      354, 360–1
   Kentucky 134–5, 269
   Livestock transporter 170,
      284–5, 286–7, 304–5
   Pneumatic 166
   Pup 78, 216–17, 322
   Reefer 72–3, 109, 150–1,
      156–7, 176, 180, 180–1, 190,
      242–3, 258–9, 263, 274–5,
      280, 286, 291, 301, 352–3,
      392–3
   Refrigerated 64, 100–1, 119,
      122, 124, 151, 163, 164–5,
      174–5, 178–9, 255, 260–1,
      278–9, 300–1, 306–7, 366,
      390–1
   Step deck 50, 243
   Storage trailer 135
   Tanker 83, 84–5, 86, 86–7, 89,

      124–5, 130, 130–1, 218–19,
      340–7, 379–81
   Van 48, 51, 52–3, 59, 66–7, 68,
      74, 90, 95, 96–7, 101, 120–1,
      122–3, 168–9, 200–1, 202,
      220–1, 228–9, 230–1, 244–5,
      246–7, 250–1, 288–9, 348–9,
      350, 357, 382–3, 392
   Walking floor 106–7, 240–1

Volvo VN series 90, 93
Volvo VN 420 100–1
Volvo VN 610 90, 94, 96
Volvo VN 660 101, 102–3, 103
Volvo VN 770 94, 96–7, 98–9

Western Star, 1987 392–3, 396–7
Western Star 4864 392
Western Star 4964, 1987 390–1
Western Star 4964 Constellation
   389
Western Star 4964EX Constellation
   394–5
Western Star 4964F 384–5, 389,
   390
Western Star 5964 388–9
Western Star Constellation 382–3,
   386–73, 392
White Freightliner CO, 1969 54–5

Acknowledgements

The style and size of this book prevented including names in most captions so I am thanking you all here. To those of you whose truck is here but not your name, know that I tried very hard, in a small percentage of cases unsuccessfully, to locate everyone. Thank you all for making American highway transport look good every day.

Alabama Motor Express; Alpha Transport; Amazon Transport/Kathy Eddy; Arambel Trucking/John Arambel; Asbury Trucking/Jerry/Allan Asbury; Atlas Bulk Carriers; Betcher Trucking/Craig Betcher; Bilik, Vladimir; Bishop, Alan/Equity Transportation; Bisom Truck Line; Bissel, Bob; Boone, Marv/Betty; Bowman, T.J.; Bradford (Kevin) & Son Trucking; Bratton, Steve; Brehmer, Greg; Brockington, Hayward; Brown, Jeff/Carol, Brown, Tom; Burke, Chris; Burns, Mike/Bonnie, C & J Express /Carla/John Nowka, C. R. England, Castiglione, Sal; Chevron DELO; Chilla, Frank; Christians, Curtis; Clark Transportation, Inc.; Classic Transportation/Jeff Tidey; Coney Island Rubbish Removal, Inc.Pioneer arting & Recycling/John Florio/Stephen Florio, Jr.; Cowen Truck Line; Crete Carriers; D&D Carting/Anthony Jr./Jack DiNardi (Tony DiNardi/Carlo DiCeglie); Davis Trucking; Delaney, Bob; DeStefano, Donnie; Dick Simon Trucking; Donton, Robert; Doucette, Mike; Dreher, Brian/Teresa, E. S. Adams and Sons Trucking; Eggleston, Rick, Ernie's Wrecker Service/Ernie Vole; Fairway Transit/Kurt Krahn; Fischer, Chris; Fisher, Hobie; Floyd, Mike; Forcelle, Fred; Foster, Dustin; G. E. Eberly & Sons, Inc.; Gary Gray Trucking/Gary Gray/Robbie Schweer; Geer, David; Gilbert, Rob; Gold, David; Golding, Geo. H., Inc./Ron Golding; Greer, Gary; Grimm, Rod/Kim; H & H Trucking/Rob Harris; Haveman Bill/Sharon; Hawkins, Virgil; Hewett, Jamie; Hicks, Nicholas/family; Hoagland, Roger/Heather; Hostetler, Jim; House, Roscoe; Huddleston, Randy; Huebner, Richard/Virginia; Hunt, Linwood; J. B. Hunt; Jeffries, Jerry/Gail; Jerry Arneson, Inc.; Job, Tod L.;John Bunning Transfer Co., Inc.; Johns, Richard; Jones, Chris/Denise; Jones, Mike/Lisa; Jones, Dan/Verda; K. L. Harring, Inc./Keith Harring; Kemner, Chuck; Kemner, Gina; Kerns, Randy; Kimball, Dan/Katie; Knezevich, Mike/Ruth; Knight, Marvin/Barbara/77 Express; Kontogouris, Ned; L. Blondeau and Sons Trucking; Lambing, Sean; Lang, Justin; Lansberry, Samuel T.; Laroue, Jody/Laurie; Laster, Robert/Dawn; Leaman, Stan; Lee Sadler & Sons; Lennon, Everett/Valerie; Leonard, A.J.; Liebman, Mike; Lily Transportation Corp.; Locklear, Kelvin/April; Lyly & Sons; MacDonald, Jack/JoAnn; Madden, Darryl; Magnum Trucking; Mahoney, Norman; Manley, Bob/Piri; Marcotte, David; Matuszak, Ken/Carol; MBH Trucking, Inc./ Matthew Brian Hitchcock; McCain, Everett; McDermon, Ed/Joanne; McGregor, George/Mickey; Miller Trucking, David Miller; Miller, Jim; Miller, Mike/Val; Morrissey, Tim; Neale, Morris; Ned Bard & Sons Company; Oak, Phil; Oxborrow Trucking, Inc./Brett Oxborrow; Patrone Trucking; Patterson Trucking/Jim Patterson; Paulson, Tom; Peter Alan & Son; Peterson, Ricky/Cindy; Peterson, Earl/Debbie; Pioneer Carting & Recycling/John Florio/Stephen Florio, Jr.; Pride Transport; Prime, Inc.; Prochnow Transport/Ron/Sky Deardorff; Putnam, W.L./Dot; Rappette, Ken/Maureen; Rayfield, Rick; Regis Beaudoin/BTC Inc.; Reliable Moving & Storage; Rhett Butler Trucking; Rhoads, Tony "Mountain Man"; Roelhof, Henry "Mr. Refuse" ; Rollman, Rick; Romanski, Robert Jr.; Salvador, Ron/Valerie ; Sanders, R. W. Jr.; Sanders, R. W. Trucking, Inc.; SantaBarbara, Tom; Schoenike, Bill ; Schott, Mike; Shacklette, Don/Donna; Sharp, Dan; Sherman, Cathy; Siegersma, Wes; Skene, Tom/Sue; Smith, Dan/Justine; Smith, Don; Smith, Gene/Hilda; Smith, Thomas ; Sorrentino Express, Inc.; Southtown Wrecker Service, Inc.; Sprague Trucking/"Wolf" McLaughlin III; Steere Tank Lines; Stempinski, Bob/Suzanne; Stenger, J. W.; Stephens, Darian; Strang Trucking, Stanley, Dannylrene; Stuck, Scott; Sunderland, Bob ; Sweeden, Buzz; Teitler, Bradley/Sparky; The Navajo Companies/Don/Karen Bartley; Thomas, Jim; Thornhill, Tim; Tigator Trucking Service; Tillamook Dairy ; Timblin, Trev; Todd, Richard; Tom Eilen & Sons Trucking/Tom, Jake, Pat/Brad Caton; Tri-State Commodities; Two B Enterprises/Jim Basse; U.S. Xpress Enterprises; Van Kampen Trucking/Marvin Van Kampen; Van Manen Oil Co.; Verdino, Blaise; W. A. Baker Trucking/Billy Baker; W. W. Pletz & Sons/Frank Roberts; Warren, Bob/Doreen; Western Distributors Transportation Corp./Dino Guadagni, Rick Walker; Western State Wholesale/Mike Humphreys; Weymouth Trucking/Melissa/Douglas Weymouth; Wilkins, Joe/Diane; Willis Shaw Express; Wyrick, Rusty; Zwald, Ken